Vij's

ELEGANT

& INSPIRED

VIKRAM VIJ
MEERU DHALWALA

PHOTOGRAPHS
BY JOHN SHERLOCK

INDIAN

CUISINE

Douglas & McIntyre
VANCOUVER/TORONTO/BERKELEY

*Vij's restaurant
is named for and dedicated to*
ROSHAN LAL VIJ,
*who lovingly pestered his young
grandson to open the
"finest restaurant in the world."*

This book is dedicated to our mothers,
Kusum Vij and Urmil (Omi) Dhalwala,
for setting up our arranged love marriage.

Douglas & McIntyre Ltd.
2323 Quebec Street, Suite 201
Vancouver, British Columbia
Canada v5t 4s7
www.douglas-mcintyre.com

Library and Archives Canada Cataloguing in Publication
Vij, Vikram, 1964–
Vij's : elegant and inspired Indian food / Vikram Vij and Meeru Dhalwala.
Includes index.
ISBN-13: 978-1-55365-184-0 · ISBN-10: 1-55365-184-7
1. Cookery, Indic. I. Dhalwala, Meeru, 1964– II. Title
TX724.5.14V53 2006   641.5954   C2006-901829-4

Editing by Lucy Kenward
Cover & text design by Naomi MacDougall and Peter Cocking
Photography by John Sherlock except for pages v, viii and 4
Photograph on p. viii (top) by Hamid Attie
Fabrics courtesy of Maiwa Handprints Ltd.
Printed and bound in Canada by Friesens
Printed on acid-free paper

We gratefully acknowledge the financial support of the
Canada Council for the Arts, the British Columbia Arts Council,
and the Government of Canada through the Book Publishing Industry
Development Program (BPIDP) for our publishing activities.

contents

above: Vikram in the original 14-seat Vij's restaurant, just after it opened in autumn 1994.

below: Vikram at age five with his mother and sister at the market in Amritsar.

ELEVEN YEARS AGO when I opened Vij's, I simply wanted to have the best Indian restaurant in Vancouver. And it was an underlying ambition of mine to increase the awareness of the cuisine, culture and country from which I came. On September 10, 1994, my parents arrived from India with a mission to "settle" their son. This involved two things: buying me a restaurant and getting me married. By December 24 of the same year, both goals were achieved.

My parents had only a three-month visa to Canada, so my dad was in a hurry. The first job was to find a location for my restaurant. One of the many spaces we saw was a fourteen-seat café and take-out place. My father liked the hustle-bustle of the busy intersection outside the café and was stuck on the fact that there would be lots of people walking by. I was adamant that I wanted to open a proper restaurant and not a casual take-out joint. My father and I debated this for a while one day, and then I left for work.

When I returned from my shift, my father informed me that he had signed and purchased the lease agreement for the café. I was speech-less. Part of me was very surprised that my father would do something so rash based on his gut feeling. The other part of me felt proud that, finally, I was the owner of my own business, no matter that it didn't meet my expectations.

As soon as I took possession of the café, I realized that it didn't have a full restaurant licence, which meant I couldn't serve liquor. Nor did it have the necessary gas hookups or exhaust system to qualify for a full licence, which meant that there would be serious restrictions on the type of cooking I could legally do there. Ever the optimists, my parents vol-unteered that they would cook the food at home and I would take these dishes to the new restaurant to sell. And this is what they did until I finally procured the appropriate kitchen licences a good three months later.

After I had run the place as the existing Middle Eastern café for a few weeks, I changed the name to Vij's and got as many personal loans as possible to carry out my new project. I reopened with a whole new menu of my own recipes. After cooking my curries at home during the day, my mother and father would take the bus to Vij's in the evening to help me clean up since I didn't have the money to hire anyone. Then we would go home, and my mother would cook dinner while my father and I had two or three whiskies and planned the next day.

At some point I decided that I shouldn't be in the back washing dishes while there were customers in the restaurant. Even if there was only one table seated at Vij's, I wanted to be out front, talking to my customers and selling my food. So, I decided to hire a part-time dishwasher during lunch hours, since that is when Vij's was busiest. I hired the first person to apply for the job, Amarjeet Gill, who is now Vij's head cook and the kitchen manager of twenty-five employees.

At the time, Amarjeet was fairly new to Canada and was as much in need of income—if not more—as I was. During the interview, I told her that initially I might not have the hours she was looking for, but that if she stuck with me during the first couple of months I would give her full-time hours. She agreed and, although I could tell that she was having trouble making ends meet, she stayed with me.

Around the same time that all this was happening, I had been introduced to Meeru over the telephone. Our mothers had been close childhood friends but they had not spoken to each other since 1965, when Meeru's parents had moved to the United States. After all these years, my mom was in North America and decided to contact her friend to see how she was doing. They talked a long time and in their excitement wanted us to say hello to one another as well. By chance, we hit it off and started to chat regularly. I could handle my parents' interest and enthusiasm over Vij's, but I couldn't handle their excitement over my talking to Meeru and their immediate hinting at our future marriage. So I kept our phone conversations to myself.

Eventually Meeru came to visit me for five days in Vancouver. She spent her days at the restaurant with Amarjeet and me. In the evenings, we would buy a bottle of wine, park my car at the Spanish Banks beach and stay there until six or seven in the morning. With my parents living with me in a small apartment (and my father still believing in a ten o'clock bedtime for all), my car was our only place for privacy. We married on December 24, 1994, soon after her trip to Vancouver. In February 1995, Meeru moved to Vancouver permanently.

She quickly became very interested and involved with our food. In fact, she was soon interfering with what we were preparing for our menu, and many discussions took place. These discussions often produced great recipes. Vij's started to get some recognition and I was invited to do interviews on television and radio. As our profile and our business increased, my landlord and the neighbouring shops complained that the smell of curry was permeating the building and interfering with their businesses. At the same time we were already realizing that, even with the appropriate licences, the kitchen wasn't equipped to accommodate our cooking requirements and our dining area was too small. So all signs pointed to getting new loans and opening a larger restaurant built on our own terms.

We were amazed how many customers took an interest in the fact that we were relocating and expanding. The most important of these was Marc Bricault, who personally designed just about every detail at Vij's—from the lamps to the pillows to our flowering ponds. Through his word of mouth we were introduced to local potters, artists, carpenters and glassblowers. Almost everything at the new restaurant was locally made by hand: our plates and bowls, lamps, tables, the bar with its intricate mosaic tiles and even our candle holders and billfolds. For us, Vij's is an Indian jewel box built by Vancouver hands.

Our recipes, developed and refined over the past ten years, are as close to our hearts as our marriage. I don't know what other newlyweds talk about, argue about or discuss for hours on end, but Meeru and I built our relationship through our recipes. Our first arguments, hurt feelings and personal accomplishments all occurred at Vij's while we were coming up with these recipes.

Our first big run-in occurred when, with a big smile, she asked me to taste her new green mango and tomato curry. Without even tasting it, I remarked that it looked like muddy mush and that I couldn't possibly serve something so ugly to my customers. She was indignant and insisted that I taste it. I conceded that it tasted great, but I still reiterated that I couldn't serve something that looked like mud. The kitchen staff still remember the incident.

Meeru and I worked for days to come up with a new recipe that tasted and looked great. And when it was all over and done with, and the curry was receiving compliments left and right, our egos got into an even larger argument over whose recipe it was! Almost twelve years later, we still compete over our recipes, only now it's at home when we cook dinner for our young daughters. Very wisely—or very shrewdly—they tell us that mama is great when she cooks and papa is great when he cooks.

Vikram Vij

above: Meeru with daughters Shanik (left) and Nanaki (right).
below: Meeru and Vikram at their wedding in December 1994.

LEVEN YEARS AGO, I was a novice at Indian cooking. I could cut meats, vegetables, onions and garlic and I knew how to sauté foods. But I had very little knowledge of what to do with spices and how to cook in "layers"—how to add and combine new and varied ingredients at different stages of the cooking process. I love it that Indian cooking can be so creative and whimsical. Even a mild curry can be full of spices in smaller quantities and be full of flavours. If you have moderate cooking experience, but are new to Indian cooking, you will be able to make most of the recipes in this book.

For us, cooking together made everything easier and more enjoyable. So I heartily recommend that you enlist a partner, relative or friend—someone who enjoys cooking—to join you in creating meals from our book. Cooking with another person and in a social environment can make any complicated recipe more interesting and fun. In Vij's kitchen, Vikram and I are surrounded by our kitchen staff, with whom we share many jokes, stories, political views and ideas. And most of these recipes have come about through talking and interacting with everyone around us.

When making these recipes the first important thing to remember, which I have stressed in various parts of the book, is that in Indian cooking, measurements aren't carved in stone. It won't really matter if you use slightly more or less of an ingredient, unless we specify otherwise in the recipe. I also encourage you to smell what you are cooking—and if you like what you smell, chances are you'll like what you've made. I now rely on my sense of smell to the point that, for the most part, I can tell if I've used too much or too little of any ingredient before I even taste the dish.

The second important thing to know is that in India a meal usually means two or three dishes shared around the table. Although we serve individual plates of food at Vij's, our intention is for our customers to share their dishes with one another. Vikram always encourages everyone at the table to order different appetizers and entrées and then share, so that there is lots of variety.

Almost all of the vegetable dishes complement any of the meat, poultry and seafood recipes. It is almost unheard of in an Indian home to serve a meat dish without a vegetarian one, even if the vegetarian dish is left over from the previous day. The sides are specifically meant to accompany any of the entrées or appetizers. In fact, an Indian meal is considered incomplete if no side dishes, such as raita, chutneys or rice, are offered. In some recipes we've mentioned specific accompaniments, but really you can pick and choose. In all recipes, we've suggested including either rice, naan or chapattis, but we encourage you to choose at least one meat, poultry or seafood dish and one vegetable or side dish when planning your meal.

At Vij's, we take great pride in the presentation of our food. After all these years, we realize that keeping garnishes to a minimum and serving the actual curries in beautiful bowls and plates is the simplest and most elegant way to serve the food.

All of our plates, bowls and dishes are handmade by local potters in a wide range of colours, shapes and sizes, which we combine to showcase our various curries. Although we are not suggesting that you go out and purchase dishes in unlimited colours, we do suggest that you take stock of what you have in the cupboard and try to match the curries to the dishes you have—much the way you complement an outfit with your accessories.

Once you've made a few of these recipes, experiment with your own combinations. Our goal is for you to become so comfortable with this book that you come up with your own serving suggestions and flavour combinations.

Meeru Dhalwala

In the Indian Kitchen

INDIAN CUISINE AND COOKING

MANY PEOPLE OUTSIDE India associate Indian food with what is essentially northern Indian and, specifically, Punjabi or tandoori cooking. Actually, the Indian food that is popular worldwide was originally *moghulai*. Milk products such as cream and yogurt, as well as nuts and raisins, were considered delicacies (and still are) in India and were an integral part of the food of the Moghuls, who ruled northern India for roughly two centuries starting with the emperor Babar in the 1500s. At this time, northern India consisted of what is now Pakistan and Bangladesh. The Moghul rulers also brought to India the tandoor, an oven originally made from clay. Breads and meats prepared in the tandoor, including kebobs or *tikkas*—marinated meats cooked on skewers—quickly became popular throughout northern India. Another menu favourite is *mukhani*, for example *dal mukhani*, which means dal cooked in butter and/or cream.

Many Indians believe that the reason for northern Indian cooking's relatively recent worldwide appeal is its popularity in their own country. Although it may not be a proven fact, the common belief is that Punjabi culture itself is highly entrepreneurial and that following the 1947 partition between India and Pakistan, many Indians emigrated to foreign countries, where some eventually opened restaurants and served versions of the food that was held in high esteem back home. As well, among the different cuisines of India, the one that most relishes meat dishes is the one descended from the Moghul dynasties. This in itself caters to North American and European tastes. Now, it's not just the Punjabis who run Indian restaurants, but the cooking at these restaurants is still for the most part northern Indian.

Within India, there are many different regions, languages and cultures with their own distinct types of "Indian" food. Instead of chapatti or naan bread, southern Indians mostly eat rice or a lentil and rice–based crepe called dosa. Many of their curries and chutneys are coconut-based. Gujaratis from the central state of Gujarat tend to finish their curries with lemon and sugar. A common joke in India is that Punjabis, like their food, are fiery, bold and loud, whereas Gujaratis, like their food, are quieter and more subtle. There is a higher percentage of vegetarians among Gujaratis than among Punjabis.

In India, goat, lamb and chicken are the meats of choice, as Hindus don't eat beef and Muslims don't eat pork. However, outside of India, many Indians serve beef and pork to meet the demands of European tastes. Our own philosophy is to keep our spices and cooking techniques Indian, while using the meats, seafood and produce that are locally available and popular. At Vij's, we have also come up with our own interpretation of Indian cuisine, which combines the spices and foods used in the different regions of India. As part of developing our own style of Indian cuisine, we have decided not to serve the traditional creamy, rich curries (butter chicken, lamb korma) or the tandoori dishes (chicken tikka masala).

In our dishes, we use only fresh vegetables. We recommend that you don't use frozen or canned vegetables for Indian cooking, as they don't retain the same texture and freshness. The one exception to this rule is frozen peas. Fresh peas are almost never available on a regular basis in North America and, if they are available, they can be prohibitively expensive. If you like peas, it is worth adding frozen ones at the very end of your cooking, even though they're not as tasty as fresh peas. Although none of our recipes here use frozen peas, you can add or substitute them in any of the vegetable dishes.

MEASURING INGREDIENTS FOR INDIAN DISHES

IT IS IMPORTANT to remember that Indian cooking is like making a pasta sauce. If you are converting these recipes from imperial to metric (page 197), you do not have to be exact in your calculations. If a recipe calls for 9 ounces or ½ pound of onions, using a little less or a little more will not ruin your recipe. You can always adjust the amount based on your personal preference. The same goes for yogurt, tomatoes, garlic, ginger and canola oil.

Almost every Indian household makes the same basic recipes; however, each one uses its own proportion of ingredients. So relax in the knowledge that unless you really use far too much or too little of the spices, you most likely will not make a bad-tasting curry. It is more important that you don't undercook your spices, which will leave a raw, harsh taste in your curry. Some spices are more flexible than others, and we will point out in the recipes which ones they are. The measurements in our recipes reflect what we cook at Vij's and what we deem to be the best balance of spices.

STAPLE INGREDIENTS

CERTAIN INGREDIENTS are integral to Indian food. Barring any allergies, these ingredients should not be excluded from a recipe, as this will alter the taste. However, true to Indian cooking's creative nature, once you are familiar with a recipe you can adjust the spicing to suit your own palate. Vikram's mother and Meeru will cook the same dish, but his mother's food will always have fewer tomatoes and less garlic. The same recipe cooked by Meeru will have more of everything. Vikram's cooking is even spicier than Meeru's. All will taste different but have the exact same ingredients, just in different quantities.

An Indian kitchen will always contain the following staple ingredients:

BASMATI RICE There is no substitute, and we recommend that you use the rice from India. It is more expensive than long-grain or jasmine rice, but the texture and fragrance of Indian basmati can't be replaced. We do not cook our basmati rice in any stock, even though some have suggested this. We find stock too heavy for the rice, destroying its soft and flaky texture. If you prefer to use brown basmati rice instead of the traditional type, there are some organic and non-organic brands available at gourmet grocers and health food stores. Remember that brown basmati takes longer to cook. It does not have the traditional basmati flavour but the grains are thinner and longer than regular long-grain brown rice.

BEANS Chickpeas are the most popular legume in Indian cooking, with kidney beans coming a close second. In fact, kidney bean curry with rice, yogurt and pickles on a Sunday afternoon is a favourite family meal across India, especially for children. In northern India, black chickpeas are also popular. They are smaller and darker and have a nuttier flavour.

CHAPATTIS There is nothing better tasting than homemade, warm chapattis, which are unleavened, flat round breads made with flour and water. All Indian grocers and markets sell premixed chapatti flour, which is a combination of bran, whole wheat and all-purpose flours. The key is to ask for chapatti flour. Chapattis are eaten daily throughout central and northern India and are also known as *roti*. It takes commitment to make chapattis at home. You will need a special flat-iron skillet called a *thava* for making them (this is discussed further in the actual recipe) and you will probably have to make several before you get the hang of it.

CHICKPEA FLOUR Also known as gram or besan flour, this flour is high in fibre and protein and has a very distinct, chickpea flavour. It is used in many Indian snacks, the most popular being pakoras (fritters) and crepes. Chickpea flour matches most Indian spices, with the exception of the Bengali panch poran, which is too pungent unless it is fried in oil first. It also goes well with dairy products such as paneer and yogurt, both of which are often used in Indian cooking. We also use it as a thickener in yogurt curry, which in India is known as just curry (pronounced *karhi*). In India, if you say you've made curry, people know that it is the yogurt-besan curry. Chickpea flour is also used in all sorts of desserts. If you don't use chickpea flour very often, store it in your refrigerator so that it keeps its flavour (refrigerated, it can be stored in an airtight container for up to 6 months).

CHILIES In addition to adding heat to a dish, chilies add flavour. We use either jalapeño peppers or serrano peppers when using fresh chilies and cayenne pepper when using dried chilies. The fresh chilies add a very slight acidic flavour in addition to the heat, whereas the dried cayenne is more pungent. How much and what type of chili you use is completely up to you and can be adjusted or deleted in any recipe according to your preferences.

CILANTRO Chopped fresh cilantro can be added to any curry. It's easy to overdo cilantro, so we pick and choose which curries we add it to. Just remember to stir it in at the very end of cooking, so it retains its flavour. Be sure to wash the cilantro in cold water. You can shake off the excess water and chop the herb for immediate use. Chop and use the stems as well as the leaves. If you are going to store it in the refrigerator, it's best to shake off the excess water, let it drain for half an hour and spread it out on a clean dishcloth. Fold the dishcloth over and gently pat dry the cilantro, then chop the herb and store it in an airtight container. Depending on the cilantro's quality and how well you dry it, it can last up to ten days in the refrigerator. (Try not to buy cilantro whose leaves are already beginning to turn brown, unless that's all you can find and you are going to cook with it that very day.)

COCONUT MILK Although coconuts are eaten as a fruit in northern India, fresh coconuts, coconut cream and coconut milk are standard in all types of South Indian cooking, from chutneys and curries to desserts. At Vij's, we use coconut milk in many of our appetizers and entrées, as it adds a different flavour and is a great substitute for yogurt or cream. Be sure to buy a high-quality coconut milk that is rich and creamy (most organic ones are of a high quality). It comes in cans, and the cream always separates from the liquid. Therefore, it is important to stir the milk before measuring it and pouring it into a curry. You may find it easier to pour the milk from the can into a bowl and use a whisk to stir it.

COOKING OIL Please do not use cooking oil replacements such as cooking sprays. Also, use the quantities recommended in the recipes, as the oil is necessary for cooking the onions, garlic and especially the spices. If you don't use enough oil or use a spray instead, the spices will taste raw in your curry. At the same time, too much cooking oil will leave your curry tasting greasy. We have used canola oil (or ghee; see below) for these recipes, as we find this to be the cooking oil that most people choose. However, you can substitute another cooking oil if you prefer.

GARLIC We are unabashed fans of garlic and, though we don't want you to omit garlic, you should feel free to decrease the amounts if you know that you or someone in your family isn't a huge fan. Make sure you have sautéed the garlic properly to a golden brown colour. If you don't sauté it enough, you will get the raw garlic flavour that lingers on your breath. If you sauté it too much, you will get a bitter taste.

GHEE Probably the most prestigious cooking oil of all is ghee, or clarified butter. It had an honoured place in the diets of the Aryans and has been in India since well before the time of the Buddha. It isn't difficult to make, and adding just a little to your curry gives it the perfect richness. The advantage of ghee is that it retains the wonderful flavour of butter (with a slightly nutty taste) but can be heated to very high temperatures without burning. Therefore, you can sauté your onions and garlic without having to worry about the butter burning and sticking to the bottom of the pan. Ghee also has a long shelf life.

So, follow the recipe in this book (page 30) and store your ghee in a Mason jar in your refrigerator. In comparison to butter, you only need to use a little ghee, so concerns that ghee is an unhealthy form of fat are unwarranted unless you overindulge.

GINGER Unless a curry specifies that ginger is the predominant flavour, the amount of this ingredient you use is completely up to you and your personal tastes. We have added it to many recipes, but feel free to change our recommendations. The more you grate or chop the ginger, the stronger its flavour will be in the curry. If you prefer a subtle ginger flavour but don't enjoy biting into the root itself, cut the ginger into big pieces, add it to your curry and remove it at the end, just before serving.

When buying ginger, make sure that you select fat pieces with unwrinkled skin. The younger the ginger looks, the juicier and better tasting it will be. The skinny, wrinkly ginger will have too many threads—we refer to them as moustaches—and won't have great flavour. The older-looking ginger will also have a more bitter taste.

LENTILS OR DAL In India, lentils are known as *dal* and are served daily. No matter which type you serve, *dal* means "lentil curry." In Punjabi, the saying "*dal, roti*" (lentil curry, bread) means the basic necessary staple meal. For a country with so many vegetarians, the various dals are an important source of protein and iron. We use the following lentils in this book:

Channa dal are also known as yellow split peas or split chickpea lentils. These dal are readily available at most non-Indian grocery stores in North America.

Mung or *moong dal* are whole green lentils. These are considered the healthiest of the lentils and are digested very easily. They don't need any soaking, and take about an hour to cook. Moong sprouts are also used in many savoury snacks.

Washed mung or *moong dal* are moong lentils split in half, with the green skin taken off. They are small yellow lentils and, of all the lentils, are the quickest to cook: they take from 20 to 25 minutes. These are not firm lentils; they are supposed to be eaten slightly mushy.

Split mung or *moong dal* are split lentils that still have the green skins on them. This distinction is very important, as the taste and texture of the washed moong and the split moong are completely different.

Masur dal are simply known as red lentils (even though they are orange) and are available in almost every grocery store in North America. These lentils are as easy to cook as the washed moong, but have a different taste and texture.

NAAN This bread originates from Central Asia and there are slight variations to it, depending on where it is eaten—Afghanistan, India, Iran or Pakistan, to name just a few countries. It is leavened bread, made from a mixture of whole wheat and all-purpose flours, and in India it is round and mostly made in a tandoor. At Vij's, we don't use a tandoor to bake our naan and it is a labour-intensive process. Since it's not easy to make naan at home, we suggest you buy it premade from Indian grocers. In Vancouver where we live, many non-Indian grocers also sell premade, prepackaged naan. We recommend that you lightly brush the heated naan with a little butter or ghee.

ONIONS Unless otherwise specified, regular yellow onions are used in our recipes. The onions in a curry take on a different flavour depending on how much you sauté them and how they are cut. For example, long slivers of onions will impart a sweeter onion flavour, and we normally cut the onions like this for a rice pilaf. The longer you sauté the onions, the stronger their flavour becomes.

TOMATOES Tomatoes are crucial to our cooking and are used in most of our curries. All curries are based on a "masala," which is the tomato, onion, garlic and spice mixture that is prepared before adding the vegetables or meats. This serves as the flavour base, or stock, for all curries. Although many drier-style curries don't need tomatoes, Meeru tends to add at least one small tomato to add a bit of juiciness. Tomatoes also help the spices cook better when sautéing the masala, and they prevent the masala from burning or sticking to the bottom of the pan.

In the winter months, tomatoes can be expensive as well as flavourless and dry. If this is the case, use canned whole tomatoes instead, but try to choose a high-quality brand, as the cheaper canned tomatoes tend to give the curry a slightly acidic taste.

YOGURT Yogurt is used in all types of Indian cooking and is also a separate accompaniment to the food. Since many curries are spicy, stirred yogurt as a side dish is a perfect cooling agent for the heat. In India, yogurt can be served with breakfast, lunch and dinner. We recommend that you use either 2% or 4% milkfat yogurt—just make sure that it is plain yogurt. Do not use soy or goat milk yogurt as a substitute in the cooking, as they alter the taste of the recipe. If you are a vegan or are lactose intolerant, you can omit the yogurt in most recipes, but remember that this will slightly alter the taste.

INDIAN HERBS AND SPICES

Below are the herbs and spices you will find in any Indian home, irrespective of the region. With these in your cupboard, you will also be able to prepare just about any simple vegetable, legume or meat curry.

CORIANDER Coriander is the seed form of green cilantro. (Fresh cilantro looks like parsley and is usually found with the fresh herbs in the produce section of the grocery store.) Ground coriander is often used with cumin and has a milder and sweeter flavour. Note that adding too much of it can give your curry a gritty texture. We also cook with the seeds, so if you have a coffee grinder, buy coriander seeds and grind them at home (page 29) when needed.

CUMIN Cumin seeds and ground cumin are both integral to our cooking. Cumin seeds give a milder flavour than ground cumin. We use ground cumin for most of our curries. However, the seeds are perfect for rice pilafs and mild vegetable side dishes. If you have a spice grinder, it is best to buy the seeds and then grind them at home (page 29) when needed.

TURMERIC The actual turmeric plant looks like a smaller version of fresh ginger. Ground, dried turmeric is used for cooking and gives curries their yellow colour. This spice has a subtle earthy or musky flavour, which can't be replaced by any other spice. Turmeric is generally reputed to be an inexpensive substitute for saffron, but we don't follow this line of thinking at all, as the two spices have different flavours. Turmeric is also considered to have many medicinal values, from strengthening the stomach and intestines to treating sprains and bruises.

AFTER CORIANDER, cumin and turmeric, the remaining Indian spices are the crown jewels in our cooking. They are the creative part of Indian cuisine, and which ones you choose and how much you use are the reasons your neighbour's meal tastes totally different from your own. Many Indian spices are renowned for their medicinal value, and many Indians use spices for preventing or treating health ailments—the most common ailments being of the stomach or intestines. Coriander, cumin and turmeric all have properties that help promote the healthy digestion of food.

Listed below are the spices we use in our recipes at Vij's and in this book, along with some practical information about how to cook with them. All these spices can be found at any Indian grocer. If you want more information or a more comprehensive list of Indian spices and their properties, there are plenty of great books that focus on the historical and botanical origins of the spices (we refer to Alan Davidson's *Oxford Companion to Food* or K.T. Achaya's *Indian Food: A Historical Companion*).

At Vij's, we buy whole, dry spices and then roast and grind them in our kitchen (pages 26–29). We find that roasting the spices deepens the flavour while getting rid of any roughness in the raw spice. By no means is it a must to pre-roast your spices; it just adds finesse and richness to the curry flavours. To roast spices, all you need is a heavy-bottomed frying pan and an exhaust fan. If you don't have time to roast all of your spices, for us, the most important ones to roast are coriander seeds, cumin seeds and fennel seeds.

AJWAIN These tiny brown seeds give a flavour similar to, yet stronger than, oregano or thyme. Ajwain is sometimes called Indian thyme. We mostly sprinkle it on our breads or add it to our fried vegetable curries. Ajwain and its essential oil are used for many medical purposes, and in the winter months our kitchen staff flavour their morning chai with ajwain to help prevent colds.

ASAFOETIDA This pungent spice is a resinous gum from a herbal plant. Also known as *hing*, it is used in minuscule amounts with vegetables, beans and lentils, but can be added to almost all curries, if you so choose. It's optional in any recipe. It tastes particularly good with turmeric, cumin seeds (ground cumin overpowers asafoetida), fenugreek seeds and mustard seeds. Although asafoetida has a pungent and strong smell, it has a mild taste. Therefore, we use asafoetida in curries that don't contain too many strong spices. Use this spice sparingly, however, or your curry will taste like medicine. Even though asafoetida is available in many forms, buy the powder, as it's much easier to cook with. Asafoetida helps to alleviate gas, constipation and stomach aches and has also has been credited with relieving toothaches, respiratory disorders such as asthma and bronchitis, and heavy and painful menstrual periods.

CARDAMOM, BLACK Black cardamoms (they are actually brown in colour) have an earthy, woody and smoky taste. Black cardamom pods look large, rough and intimidating next to their dainty green cousins. They are also less expensive and, unfairly, not as cherished a spice. If you peel back the rough skin of black cardamom pods, you will find beautiful, moist dark-brown seeds inside. These seeds carry the flavour, and you can discard the pod. Our garam masala (page 26) wouldn't be the same without black cardamom seeds.

As with cinnamon and cloves, we don't pre-roast black cardamom seeds unless we are roasting them with the other whole spices in our garam masala.

CARDAMOM, GREEN Green cardamoms are little light-green pods with dark brown seeds inside. The darker the seeds, the riper the pod. Avoid using pods with light brown seeds, as these carry little to no flavour. We use green cardamom to flavour our chai and desserts. Indians chew on a green cardamom pod as a breath freshener. There is no need to roast green cardamom.

CAYENNE We use dried whole, crushed or ground cayenne chilies, depending on how we want the curry to look. Whole cayenne chilies can look quite beautiful in a drier-style vegetable curry. Cayenne is strong and pungent, and most Indians will use at least a little in all their curries. Many of the regional cuisines make a cayenne paste by pounding the peppers with a little water or oil in a mortar. You can buy all types of dried cayenne peppers at any Indian grocer, and most other grocery stores carry ground cayenne pepper.

CINNAMON We use only cinnamon bark, unless it is ground in garam masala. Ground cinnamon on its own can easily overpower the flavour of an entire curry. There is no need to pre-roast cinnamon bark, unless you are using it for garam masala (page 26).

CLOVES We use only whole cloves and take them out at the end of cooking, unless they are ground in garam masala. As with cinnamon, adding even slightly too much ground cloves can ruin your curry. Many Indians chew cloves to soothe and relieve toothaches and painful gums.

CURRY LEAVES It's not always easy to buy fresh curry leaves in North America, but they give a wonderful, nutty, "curry" flavour. Curry leaves are so abundant in India that many vegetable vendors give customers free bunches with their vegetables. Most cooks in India add curry leaves to their curries at random, as the leaves go with just about any spice combination. If you find fresh curry leaves at your Indian grocer, make sure they are a deep green colour and give off a "curry" smell. If the leaves have a brownish tinge or are brown, they have gone bad and will be of no use to you. You don't need to wash curry leaves, but if you do, make sure you place them on a towel and dry them completely before you start cooking with them. Keep a safe distance from the pan when you fry curry leaves in oil, as water from within the leaves can sometimes splatter! (The water means the leaves are very fresh and very flavourful.)

FENNEL We don't cook many savoury dishes with fennel seeds, although there are a few in this book. For the most part, fennel seeds are eaten as an after-dinner digestive, used as a breath freshener or added to give an anise-like flavour to Indian pickles, chai and certain desserts. A staple after-dinner recipe is to mix ½ cup roasted fennel seeds with ½ cup coarse white sugar. Indians usually take a teaspoon of this and eat it a little at a time. We roast fennel seeds before eating them, as roasting brings out the anise flavour and gets rid of the grassy texture of unroasted fennel seeds.

FENUGREEK LEAVES Dried, green fenugreek leaves add a flavour similar to that of celery. They have a much earthier taste than fenugreek seeds and should be sprinkled into a curry at the very end of the cooking process. They taste great in cream-based and/or meat curries. In Indian stores, be sure to purchase kasuri methi (*methi* means "fenugreek leaves," and Kasur is a northern region famous for its *methi*). Be careful not to confuse green fenugreek leaves with the yellow fenugreek seeds in a recipe.

FENUGREEK SEEDS We prefer to grind fenugreek seeds coarsely rather than use whole seeds when cooking. It can be difficult to buy ground fenugreek seeds, so this is one spice that requires some work in a coffee/spice grinder. When ground, these seeds give the "curry" flavour that many associate with curry powder, without the bitter taste that comes from biting into the whole seeds. If you use too many or overcook either whole or ground fenugreek seeds, they become quite bitter.

GARAM MASALA We make our own garam masala (page 26) at Vij's, and this is the signature spice that distinguishes our curries from many others. *Garam* means "warm," and the spices in this masala take on the same warm connotation as the spices in a hot cider. Our garam masala is 80 per cent ground cumin, and the remaining spices are cinnamon, cloves, the seeds from black cardamom, nutmeg and mace. For the recipes in this book, we urge you to make our garam masala. Once made, one batch will keep up to 6 months in your cupboard, as long as it is in an airtight container. If you use a different garam masala, remember that your curry may not have the same taste as ours.

KALONJI Also known as *nigella*, these small charcoal-coloured seeds will give a toasted onion flavour to your curry. Kalonji is also used to flavour mango pickle, especially in conjunction with fennel, as these two spices complement one another very well.

MACE We use mace in our garam masala only, along with nutmeg.

MANGO POWDER This powder is made from unripe or green mangoes that are sundried then ground. When cooked, mango powder, which is known as *amchur* in Hindi, gives a mild, sweet and tangy flavour. We use it in our mild curries or when we're making a child-friendly curry. Mango powder is also a staple spice in *chaat*, a very popular and healthy salad served as a snack. Fruit chaats are made with fresh fruit, lemon, salt and mango powder. Other chaats are made with moong lentils, potatoes and chips made from chickpea flour.

MEXICAN CHILI POWDER This spice mixture is usually used in tacos and Mexican chili, but it also goes well with some Indian curries. It is a combination of red chilies, paprika and cumin, depending on the brand you buy. We use a Mexican chili powder that is a deeper brick colour, which means it has less cumin in it. This is not a very hot spice.

MUSTARD SEEDS We use black or dark brown mustard seeds. When fried in oil for 1 to 2 minutes, mustard seeds impart a slightly nutty flavour. After 1 to 2 minutes, you will hear a popping sound, which means that the seeds have cooked and are beginning to burn. At this point, quickly add other ingredients to the seeds or remove from the heat. Fully burned mustard seeds are very bitter. We also grind mustard seeds and use the ground seeds in a few curries. When ground, the seeds give a slightly tart flavour. Like asafoetida, mustard seeds—ground or whole—should be used only when cooking with a few spices, so the flavour of the seeds comes through.

NUTMEG We use nutmeg in our garam masala only, along with mace.

PANCH PORAN This is a Bengali five-spice mixture, just as garam masala is a Punjabi spice mixture. Unlike garam masala, which is a blend of ground spices, panch poran is normally sold as premixed whole seeds. It consists of fenugreek seeds, kalonji, fennel, yellow or black mustard seeds and cumin seeds. Whether ground or used whole, panch poran needs to be cooked in hot oil or ghee for 30 to 40 seconds before anything else is added, otherwise the raw pungency of these spices remains in the curry. We buy panch poran with yellow mustard seeds, roast the seeds and then grind the mixture to use in our curries (page 28).

PAPRIKA We use paprika only for aesthetic reasons. Sometimes the combination of spices in a dish will result in a light brown or yellow colour, and we will add paprika just to spruce up the colour without altering the taste of the curry.

POMEGRANATE SEEDS Pomegranates are very popular in the Middle East and in South Asia. The deep red pulp, which is what makes the fruit such a delicacy, surrounds the small seeds, which are either swallowed or spat out while eating the fruit. The best fruit has soft seeds that are easily chewed and swallowed. Wild pomegranate trees bear pomegranates with very little of the sweet red pulp and mostly the seeds. In India, these wild pomegranates—which cannot be eaten as a fruit—are dried and used as a sour condiment or spice. At Indian grocers, pomegranate seeds are known as *anardana*.

RAW SUGAR Known as *gur*, this sweetener is sugar cane juice boiled down to a coarse, brown sugar. You can buy it only at an Indian grocer. If you can, buy the raw sugar that is crumbly and not in hard pellets. To get the same flavour, you can substitute demerara sugar, but it will be more expensive. Make sure that you are purchasing real demerara sugar, which is a partly refined, more golden-coloured sugar. Many cheaper demerara sugars are made with molasses and don't have the same, rich taste.

SAFFRON As elsewhere in the world, in India true saffron is the most expensive and cherished spice. You need to use only a very little to give off its aroma. If you use too much, rather than getting more of a good thing, you end up wasting money and rendering your food bitter and pungent. Saffron doesn't go well with many of the stronger Indian spices, so it is used mainly in mild curries and desserts.

SALT, BLACK Black salt is actually pink in colour and has a sulphuric smell. It comes mostly from Pakistan and parts of northern India. Although it is not usually used as a cooking salt, we sprinkle it on deep-fried foods to give them a slightly tart and pungent flavour.

TAMARIND We cook with a tamarind paste that we make from boiling tamarind pulp and then straining it (page 32). You can buy tamarind pulp, as well as ready-made tamarind paste, at all Indian grocers. We prefer to buy the pulp and boil and strain it ourselves, as it is a purer form of the paste and has a stronger flavour. It is usually used to provide a tart and acidic taste.

Basics

GARAM MASALA

1 heaping tsp whole cloves

1½ tsp black cardamom seeds (about 10 whole cardamom pods)

6 heaping Tbsp cumin seeds

1 Tbsp pounded cinnamon sticks

¼ tsp ground mace

¼ tsp ground nutmeg

GARAM MEANS "WARM" and masala means "spices," and many of our dishes depend on this particular recipe. All regional cooking in India has its own version of this spice, though it is often called by other names. Other regional spice mixtures may be more pungent or hot and spicy, but all versions of garam masala tend to have a sweetness to them.

When we first opened Vij's, in fall 1994, we used store-bought ground spices. In our chicken curry for twenty servings, we used eight table-spoons of garam masala. Six months later, we started buying whole spices and sifting, roasting and grinding them ourselves. For the same chicken curry, we used five tablespoons of our own garam masala. The colour of the chicken curry changed from a lighter to a deeper brown, and the texture became less gritty. So, although the previous chicken curry tasted fine (in retrospect, not nearly as good), our second chicken curry required less of each spice but resulted in a dish with a stronger, richer flavour and a more velvety texture.

It's really not difficult to sift, roast and grind your spices, though it will take you about an hour. If you do cook Indian food on a regular basis, it's worth your time. You just need a spice or coffee grinder (that you use only for grinding spices) and a small heavy-bottomed frying pan.

With a little creativity, a well-made garam masala can be added to many non-Indian dishes to give them that special, exotic flavour. (We have a close friend who sprinkles it on her pizza!) The key is that the spices for garam masala have to be pre-roasted, as this cooks each one and brings it to its peak of flavour. Many store-bought garam masala mixtures aren't roasted and tend to have a dull flavour.

All the whole spices listed below are available from most Indian grocers. The aroma from the roasting will be quite strong. Therefore, ensure you have appropriate ventilation in your home. At a minimum, close all bedroom and bathroom doors and keep your kitchen exhaust fan on.

Makes ¾ cup

TURN ON YOUR stovetop exhaust fan. In a heavy-bottomed frying pan, heat cloves, black cardamom seeds, cumin seeds and cinnamon sticks on medium to high heat, stirring constantly. When the cumin seeds become a darker shade of brown, remove from the stove. Transfer the roasted spices to a bowl and cool for 20 minutes.

Place roasted spices, mace and nutmeg in a spice (or coffee) grinder and grind until the mixture has the consistency of store-bought ground black pepper. Can be used right away. Will also keep in an airtight container in a dark cupboard or drawer for up to 6 months.

PANCH PORAN

3½ oz panch poran seeds

WHAT GARAM MASALA is to Punjabis, panch poran is to Bengalis. This spice mixture is made up of fenugreek seeds, kalonji, fennel, yellow or black mustard seeds and cumin seeds. It is difficult to buy premixed ground panch poran, but you can buy premixed whole panch poran seeds at most Indian grocers and then grind them at home in a coffee or spice grinder. Roast the entire package of seeds (the smallest size packet available is 3½ ounces/100 grams), grind them and store any leftover ground panch poran. This is a pungent mixture, so be sure to close all bedroom and bathroom doors, and to keep your kitchen exhaust fan on, while roasting the spices.

Makes ½ cup

TURN ON YOUR stovetop exhaust fan. Heat a small, heavy-bottomed frying pan on medium-high heat for 1 minute. Add panch poran, stirring constantly for 2 to 3 minutes, or until the mixture darkens. Transfer roasted seeds to a bowl and cool for 15 minutes.

Place roasted seeds in a spice (or coffee) grinder and grind to the consistency of store-bought ground black pepper. Can be used right away. Will also keep in an airtight container in a dark cupboard or drawer for up to 6 months.

CUMIN AND CORIANDER

W E HIGHLY RECOMMEND that you sift and roast whole cumin and coriander and store the seeds, separately, in airtight containers. Then, if a recipe calls for ground cumin or coriander, you can grind the roasted seeds in a spice (or coffee) grinder just before cooking them.

Depending on the quality of the cumin and the coriander, you may need to sift the seeds before you grind them. Discard any small rocks and clumps of dirt you find. For the past ten years, we have been buying the same brands of cumin and coriander; we find we get more rocks at some times than others. Typically we also find more dirt and rocks while sifting the coriander.

One tablespoon of whole cumin seeds will yield 1 tablespoon of ground cumin. Two tablespoons of coriander seeds will yield 1½ tablespoons of ground coriander.

Makes 1 cup cumin and ¾ cup coriander

1 cup cumin seeds, sifted

1 cup coriander seeds, sifted

CUMIN Heat a 10-inch heavy-bottomed frying pan on medium-high heat for 1 minute. Add cumin seeds, and stirring regularly, cook for 3 to 4 minutes, or until darker in colour. Pour roasted seeds onto a plate and cool for 20 minutes. Can be used right away. Will also keep in an airtight container in a dark cupboard or drawer for up to 6 months.

CORIANDER Heat a 10-inch heavy-bottomed frying pan on medium-high heat for 1 minute. Add coriander seeds, and stirring regularly, cook for 3 to 4 minutes, or until seeds look slightly burned on one side. Pour roasted seeds onto a plate and cool for 20 minutes. Can be used right away. Will also keep in an airtight container in a dark cupboard or drawer for up to 6 months.

GHEE

(CLARIFIED BUTTER)

1 lb unsalted butter

THERE IS NO substitute for ghee in Indian cooking. It is easy to make, has its own distinct nutty flavour and, most importantly, can be heated to high temperatures without burning. We highly recommend that you use ghee for the recipes in this book.

We use ghee like butter, but in smaller quantities. If you like ghee, you can always use it in place of canola oil. Or you can use half ghee, half oil to make up the required amount of oil in a recipe. We usually start with unsalted butter, but you can also use the salted variety. The salt will just burn slightly and drop to the bottom of the pan once the ghee is made. Just be sure to leave the salt in the bottom of the pan when you pour off the ghee. The entire process, from solid butter to ghee, should take 15 to 18 minutes. If you are vegan or lactose intolerant, you can omit ghee in most recipes.

Makes 1⅓ cups

MELT BUTTER in a small, heavy pot on medium heat. Once melted, reduce the heat slightly and boil gently for 5 minutes. Using a small sieve, scoop out the solids that are floating on top. Continue gently boiling butter and scooping the floating solids every 3 minutes. Scoop carefully so you remove only the solids and not the actual ghee that is forming. You will notice the butter change slowly from a creamy light yellow to a clear golden liquid with fewer solids. After 10 to 13 minutes the ghee will start to foam. Using the sieve, scoop through the foam to make sure you have removed all of the solids. Once the foam reduces, you will have a clear golden liquid. This is ghee. Turn off the heat and allow ghee to cool for about 20 minutes.

Pour ghee into a jar with a tight-fitting lid. Once it is completely cool, refrigerate ghee. Can be used right away. Will keep refrigerated in an airtight container for 3 months (or longer).

TOMATO BROTH

W E USE THIS tomato broth for our seafood and chicken dishes. It adds a mild, tart tomato base to a curry. We also use this broth for curries that are light on the spices. It does, however, taste great with lots of ground cayenne pepper.

Makes 3½ cups

4 lbs tomatoes

6 cups water

PLACE TOMATOES and water in a pot. Cover and bring to a boil on high heat. Immediately reduce the heat to low and simmer for 1 hour. Remove from the heat and allow to cool.

Place a fine-mesh sieve with handles over a large pot, positioning it so there is space between the bottom of the sieve and the bottom of the pot. Using a large ladle or a cooking spoon, carefully transfer the tomato mixture to the sieve. Press tomatoes to extract as much liquid as possible. Discard tomato skins and reserve the tomato broth. Can be used right away. Will also keep refrigerated for 1 week or frozen for up to 1 month in a sealed container.

TAMARIND PASTE

2½ cups water

1 packet (14 oz) pure seedless tamarind ("imli")

I'S BETTER TO make your own tamarind paste than to buy it ready-made from the grocery store, as this recipe is pure tamarind and water. All of our recipes are based on this particular tamarind paste recipe. Since tamarind is used in many Asian cuisines, you can buy it at most Asian grocers. At an Indian grocer, packets of concentrated tamarind pulp may be labelled "imli." You may wish to wear multi-purpose latex gloves if you use your hands to mash the tamarind paste through the strainer, as it's sticky and the dark paste can get stuck under your nails.

Makes 1¾ cups

COMBINE WATER and tamarind in a small pot and bring to a boil on high heat. Reduce the heat to medium and boil tamarind for 10 minutes, using a large spoon to mash and break tamarind in small pieces. You will notice some hard pieces that cannot be mashed. Remove the mixture from the stove and cool in the pot for half an hour or until lukewarm.

Place a fine-mesh sieve over a bowl. Strain the tamarind mixture, using your hands or the back of a metal spoon to mash solids through the sieve and into the bowl until all that is left are pieces of tough skin. Discard these skins. The resulting paste should have the consistency of puréed baby food.

Can be used right away. Will keep refrigerated for up to 5 days or frozen for up to 3 months in an airtight container.

SIMPLE MASALA

I N HINDI, THE word "masala" has two important meanings that are linked. First, masala(s) means "spice(s)," both individually and when a dry spice mixture is made. So, cumin is a masala and garam masala (a mixture of various ground spices such as cumin, cloves and cinnamon) is also a masala. Second, masala also refers to the spices cooked in an onion-garlic-tomato mixture which you prepare before adding your meats, vegetables or legumes, and which is used for most Indian curries. One Indian might ask another, for example, "What did you put in your masala?" or "Did you put yogurt in your masala?" This is your *wet* masala and it serves as the flavour base or stock for your curry.

There are simple masala bases for your curry and there are more complicated ones. Both can be equally delicious. Vikram's parents eat only curries based on a simple masala: they use just a small amount of onions and tomatoes with a touch of turmeric, cumin seeds and salt. Meeru's parents eat curries based on spicy, more complex masalas: her mother will use up to ten different spices with lots of onions, garlic, ginger and tomatoes. At Vij's, we try to serve a balance of both.

If you are preparing Indian cuisine for the first time, follow this recipe several times until you feel comfortable with the process. After making this masala, you can add any vegetable to it, except for broccoli. Broccoli is one non-Indian vegetable whose flavours, in our view, don't match Indian spices. Not all Indians share this view.

Serves 2 to 3

⅓ cup canola oil

1½ cups finely chopped onions (2 medium)

2 Tbsp chopped garlic

1½ cups chopped tomatoes (2 medium-large)

½ tsp turmeric

2 tsp ground cumin

1½ tsp ground coriander

1½ tsp salt

½ tsp ground cayenne pepper (optional)

1 can (14 oz) chickpeas or kidney beans, rinsed and drained

1 to 2 cups water

HEAT OIL in a heavy-bottomed pot on medium-high heat. Add onions and sauté until golden brown, 5 to 8 minutes. Add garlic and sauté until browned, about 3 more minutes. Stir in tomatoes, then add turmeric, cumin, coriander, salt and cayenne (if desired). Turn down the heat to medium and sauté, stirring regularly, until the oil separates from this masala mixture. This means the spices are cooked through and the "stock" for your curry is made.

So that you don't waste this masala, add chickpeas (or kidney beans) and enough water to make a curry with a consistency you prefer. (Adding all the water will make a soupy curry.) Stir well, cover and bring to a boil. Reduce the heat to low and simmer for about 5 minutes. Your basic curry is ready to eat.

PANEER

PANEER IS A mild Indian cheese made from whole milk. It tastes great raw, cooked in curries, and marinated and grilled. Since it is mild, it's popular with children as well as adults. It is fairly easy to make, but it can taste like burned milk if the milk is heated in a light pan on high heat. According to Punjabi village folklore, if you pour a little bit of water in the pan before adding the milk, you will prevent the milk from sticking to the bottom of the pan and burning. (Our kitchen staff insisted that I add that tip to this recipe, as this is what they still do at Vij's.)

Because the right type of cheesecloth and pan are crucial to making a good paneer, they are listed as part of the ingredients. Make sure you use three layers of cheesecloth, either by placing three single layers on top of each other or by folding the cheesecloth in thirds so it makes a triple layer. If you use a single layer, too much of the milk solids will be strained with the liquid. Although you can buy paneer in most Indian grocers, at home you can make preservative-free paneer with organic milk. Make sure you use whole milk.

For a simple dessert or a snack, keep the paneer soft by placing the two-quart pan of water over the wrapped paneer for only ten minutes. It will have the consistency of cottage cheese. Unwrap the paneer, add honey, maple syrup or sugar and enjoy.

Makes about 1½ pounds

PLACE WATER in the large heavy-bottomed pan. Slowly add milk, then stir in sugar. Turn the heat to medium and bring milk to a boil. This will take about 15 minutes. *Do not* leave milk unattended on the stove, as it expands quickly and may overflow. Just as the milk rises, but before it spills over the side of the pot, add vinegar and turn off the heat. The milk will stop rising, and solids will begin to separate from the liquid. Wait 5 minutes until the liquid is completely separated from the solids.

Line a fine-mesh sieve with triple-layered cheesecloth and place it in the sink. Strain the milk mixture through the cheesecloth, leaving the paneer in the sieve for about 5 minutes to drain completely. Using your hands, gather the edges of the cheesecloth, bringing them together above the paneer. Enclose paneer tightly in the cheesecloth by twisting the gathered edges against the paneer to seal out any air. Tie the gathered ends into a double knot.

Fill a 2-quart pot with water. Place wrapped paneer on a large plate and set the pot of water on top. This will flatten the paneer to about 2 inches thick, pressing out the remaining water and making the cheese thicker. Allow paneer to sit for 1 hour.

Unwrap paneer, using a spoon to scrape any cheese stuck to the cheesecloth, and place it on a clean plate. With a large sharp knife, cut paneer according to your recipe.

Can be used right away. Will keep, uncut and tightly sealed in plastic wrap or a resealable plastic bag, refrigerated for up to 4 days.

¼ cup water

1 gallon whole milk

1½ tsp granulated sugar

⅓ cup white vinegar

3 squares of cheesecloth, each 2 ft × 2 ft, or 1 larger square folded in thirds

1 large heavy-bottomed pan

SPICED, ROASTED

ALMONDS OR CASHEWS

THERE ARE HUNDREDS of variations to this recipe. If you don't have any garam masala, you can substitute ground cumin. It will just have a different flavour. We serve roasted nuts in a bowl as hors d'oeuvres with drinks. We also use six to eight roasted cashews as a garnish with paneer and vegetable curries and a similar number of roasted almonds as a garnish for our meat curries.

You have to roast the nuts at a high temperature, but you don't want to burn them. So, keep a close watch on the cashews especially, as they burn easily. We've listed the temperature as 375°F based on our commercial-strength oven. However, you may have to adjust the temperature slightly higher or lower depending on your own oven. Be sure to cool the nuts completely before serving them, as the warm nuts are chewy and unappealing.

Makes 1 lb

1 lb whole raw almonds or cashews

2 Tbsp canola oil

1 Tbsp salt

½ Tbsp mango powder

1 Tbsp garam masala (page 26) or ground cumin

½ Tbsp ground cayenne pepper

PREHEAT THE OVEN to 375°F. In a large bowl, thoroughly combine almonds (or cashews), oil, salt, mango powder, garam masala (or cumin) and cayenne. Spread the coated almonds (or cashews) on a baking tray. (You can mix the nuts, oil and spices directly on the baking tray if you prefer.) Bake almonds for 5 to 8 minutes (or cashews for 4 to 5 minutes). Lightly toss almonds (or cashews) to distribute the spices evenly and ensure they don't burn. Return almonds to the oven for 5 to 8 minutes more (or cashews for 4 to 5 minutes more), until slightly darker. If they turn dark brown at the edges, they are about to burn. Remove almonds (or cashews) from the oven and allow to cool completely, 45 minutes to 1 hour, before serving.

Can be used right away. Will keep for up to 1 month in an airtight container in a cool, dry place.

On the Table

Appetizers & Salads

Curried Chicken Liver Pâté 42

Warm Eggplant, Onion and Tomato Salad 43

Turmeric and Saffron Curry 44

Tomato, Coriander and Ginger Soup 45

Sautéed Arugula and Spinach
with Paneer and Roasted Cashews 47

Mango and Tomato Curry 48

Curried Brussels Sprouts with Paneer and Bacon 49

Sautéed Brussels Sprouts,
Red Bell Peppers, Paneer and Cashews 50

Garam Masala–sautéed Portobello
Mushrooms in Porcini Cream Curry 52

Jalapeño and Cumin-spiced Paneer and Couscous Cakes 53

Seasonal Vegetables with Grated
Coconut and Black Chickpea Rice 55

Potato and Cauliflower Pakoras (Fritters) 57

Potato Pooris 60

Prawns in Coconut Masala 63

Beef Kebobs with Creamy Bengali-style Curry 64

Grilled Lamb or Mutton Kebobs 66

CURRIED CHICKEN LIVER PÂTÉ

½ cup canola oil

½ tsp asafoetida

½ lb red onions, finely chopped (1 medium)

1 tsp garam masala (page 26)

½ tsp ground fenugreek seeds

½ tsp ground cayenne pepper

¼ tsp turmeric

1 tsp salt

1 cup puréed tomatoes (2 large)

1 lb chicken livers, washed

1½ oz kale leaves, washed and finely chopped

3 Tbsp dry white wine

1 box sturdy crackers

INDIANS TRADITIONALLY DON'T eat pâté, so this pâté is a European dish which we have prepared Indian style, using Indian ingredients. It tastes great with our potato *pooris* (page 60). Any leftover pâté will keep, refrigerated in a sealed container, for 2 to 3 days.

The asafoetida adds a subtle flavour to this dish. The word literally means stinking resin, and it does have a pungent smell but don't be put off. It's milder when cooked. Meeru's mother tells a story of how Indians discovered this spice. Thousands of years ago, people noticed that whenever a cow was in distress, it would lick the roots of this particular plant and look visibly relieved. So they deduced that something in the roots of this plant made the cow feel better. Since then, asafoetida has been used as an elixir for flatulence and all stomach-related ailments.

Kale smoothes out the flavours of the livers and the Indian spices, and although you can't actually taste it in this recipe, you must add it. One bunch of kale usually has 7 to 8 stalks. To get the right amount for this dish, take about 3 large stalks and tear off the kale leaves. It doesn't matter if you're slightly off on the amount.

Serves 6

HEAT OIL in a medium pot on high heat for 1 minute. Add asafoetida and cook for 10 seconds. Add onions, reduce the heat to medium and sauté for 5 to 8 minutes, or until golden to medium brown. Add garam masala, fenugreek, cayenne, turmeric and salt. Stir well, then cook for 3 minutes. Stir in tomatoes and cook for another 10 minutes, until the oil glistens on top.

Stir in chicken livers and kale leaves and cook for 8 to 10 minutes, stirring gently but regularly. Once chicken livers harden a bit and stop bleeding during the cooking process, they are cooked. Remove from the stove and cool for 45 minutes.

In a food processor, combine the chicken liver mixture and white wine. Purée until smooth. Transfer to a stainless steel or glass bowl, cover with plastic wrap and refrigerate for at least 1 hour.

TO SERVE Scoop the pâté into a glass or ceramic bowl. Set the bowl on a serving tray and arrange the crackers around the bowl.

WINE At Vij's we always recommend a Riesling Auslese with this pâté.

WARM EGGPLANT

ONION AND TOMATO SALAD

T HIS IS A light dish that goes well with couscous or rice, or even with organic greens as a salad. When buying eggplants, compare eggplants of the same size and select the ones that weigh less. This has been the tradition for generations in both our families, as this increases the chances of getting eggplants with more "meat" and fewer seeds. Most of the ingredients are the same as for the Eggplant, Tomato and Green Onion Curry (page 131), but this dish is prepared differently.

Serves 6 to 8

3 large eggplants in ½-inch rounds

1½ tsp salt

1 tsp ground cayenne pepper

2 large onions, in thick slivers

6 Tbsp canola or olive oil

1 tsp mango powder

1 large tomato, in large chunks

PREHEAT THE OVEN to 350°F. In a large shallow roasting pan, combine eggplants, salt, cayenne, onions and oil. Mix thoroughly, then bake on the middle rack for 25 minutes, or until eggplant is tender. Remove from the oven and immediately add mango powder and tomato chunks while still hot. Mix well and serve.

TO SERVE Divide warm eggplant salad among bowls. If serving with couscous or rice, pour warm eggplant over equal portions in large bowls.

WINE This salad is great with a glass of Prosecco (Italy) or Cava (Spain).

TURMERIC AND SAFFRON CURRY

½ tsp saffron

½ cup warm water
for saffron

⅓ cup canola oil

3 Tbsp all-purpose flour

4 Tbsp crushed
canned tomatoes

¾ cup plain yogurt, stirred

2 tsp salt

½ tsp turmeric

3½ cups water

1 Tbsp white rice vinegar

W E JOKINGLY REFER to this as our Hindu curry—orange being the colour of marigolds, the clothing of Hindu priests and the markings on temple doors. This is a very light and mild curry, and we prefer to eat it as a broth on its own. It's a great precursor to a spicier main dish.

Try to use saffron with dark orange strings. The yellow strings of saffron have very little flavour and often taste stale. As for the vinegar, use only rice vinegar, since it is milder and has a different flavour than regular vinegar. You can use the leftover rice vinegar in salads where you would use oil and vinegar.

The key to this recipe is constant stirring. It will take you no more than fifteen minutes to make this dish.

Serves 6

COMBINE SAFFRON and the ½ cup water in a small bowl. Soak for 15 minutes.

Heat oil in a medium pot on medium heat. Add flour, stirring continuously and cooking for about 5 minutes, or until flour is orange/tan. Reduce the heat to low and add tomatoes and yogurt. Stir well to combine, then add salt and turmeric. Cook for another minute. Add the 3½ cups water and the saffron and its water, stir well and increase the heat to medium-high. Bring to a boil, stir again and turn off the heat. Stir in rice vinegar.

TO SERVE Serve hot in small soup bowls.

WINE No wine, but perhaps some sparkling water.

TOMATO, CORIANDER AND GINGER SOUP

WE HAVE ALWAYS served this soup with our vegetable pakoras (page 57)—first as an appetizer at Vij's and now as a light lunch at Rangoli (our café and market). We place 5 or 6 pakoras in a bowl and pour the soup over them. Of course, you can eat it on its own with naan or a baguette. You can also sauté your own vegetables and add them to the soup.

If you are not a fan of ginger, make this soup with garlic instead. Indians prefer ginger, as garlic is used in just about everything else. Choose garlic or ginger, since using both will hide the flavour of the coriander seeds. Similarly, use curry leaves or cilantro but do not use both. Curry leaves will give the soup more of a "curry" flavour, whereas cilantro will add a light freshness at the end. In the winter we use curry leaves and in the summer we use cilantro. Be sure to buy green curry leaves without any brownish tinges—good curry leaves smell like curry. Also be sure to use juicy tomatoes so you get a rich tomato taste.

Serves 6

⅓ cup canola oil

¼ tsp asafoetida

1 Tbsp + 1 tsp cumin seeds

15 to 20 curry leaves (optional)

1 oz ginger or 1 oz garlic, peeled and thinly sliced

1 Tbsp + 1 tsp ground coriander

1 tsp crushed cayenne pepper

1½ tsp salt

3 cups puréed tomatoes (6 large)

6 cups water or 3 cups water and 3 cups chicken stock

½ cup whipping cream (optional)

½ cup chopped cilantro

IN A LARGE POT, heat oil for 1 minute on medium-high heat. Add asafoetida, cumin seeds and curry leaves and allow to sizzle for 30 seconds. (Be careful of any water splattering from within the curry leaves.) The curry leaves will begin to shrivel. Add ginger (or garlic) and stir well. (If you are using garlic, sauté it for 2 to 3 minutes until golden brown.) Reduce the heat to medium and add coriander, cayenne and salt. Stir and sauté for 5 minutes.

Add tomatoes and water (or water and chicken stock). Stir well, cover and bring to a boil. Reduce the heat to medium-low and simmer for half an hour. For a richer soup, stir in cream. Just before serving, stir in cilantro.

TO SERVE Ladle soup into six individual bowls.

WINE A rich Viognier/Roussanne blend provides a perfect balance with the tomatoes. Washington State is producing great such Rhône-style blends.

SAUTÉED ARUGULA AND SPINACH

WITH PANEER AND ROASTED CASHEWS

W E USE ABOUT one-quarter arugula to three-quarters spinach. Too much arugula will make this dish bitter. Sometimes it is difficult to get arugula and we substitute rapini (known as Italian broccoli or Chinese gai lan); then we use half rapini and half spinach. This dish tastes particularly great with naan, as the bread soaks up the rich curry nicely.

Serves 6

PREHEAT THE OVEN or toaster oven to 375°F. Spread cashews on a baking tray and bake for 3 minutes. Gently stir cashews to roast them evenly. Return to the oven for another 3 minutes, or until golden brown. Watch carefully because cashews can burn quickly. Remove from the oven and cool for at least 30 minutes.

Cut the tougher, bottom stems (about 1½ inches) off the spinach. If you don't like to eat the stems, cut off all of them but add more spinach leaves to compensate. If the rapini leaves are flowering on top, cut off the flowers. Cut off the bottom stems of the rapini. If you don't eat any of the rapini stems, cut off as much as you want, but again compensate with extra rapini leaves. Combine spinach and arugula (or rapini) in a large bowl.

Heat oil in a large frying pan on medium-high heat for 1 minute. Add cumin seeds, stir and allow to sizzle for 30 to 45 seconds. Add tomatoes, mustard seeds, turmeric, salt and cayenne. Stir and reduce the heat to low, then cover and cook for 5 minutes. Remove the lid and stir. The top of the masala should glisten with oil. If not, cook uncovered for another 1 to 2 minutes to make sure the spices are cooked through.

Stir in water and increase the heat to medium. Bring to a boil, then reduce the heat to low and cook at a low boil for 5 to 8 minutes. Add coconut milk, increase the heat to medium and continue cooking until the curry starts to boil. Add greens and cook them for 2 minutes, stirring regularly.

TO SERVE Place 2 slices of paneer in each of six large bowls. Pour the curry and green leaves over the paneer. Top the greens with 6 to 7 roasted cashews per bowl.

WINE Pair with a refreshing Grüner Veltliner.

2 oz whole raw unsalted cashews

½ lb arugula + 1½ lbs spinach or 1 lb rapini + 1 lb spinach

½ cup canola oil

1 Tbsp cumin seeds

3 cups puréed tomatoes (9 medium)

1 Tbsp + 1 tsp ground black mustard seeds

½ tsp turmeric

1 Tbsp salt

1 tsp crushed cayenne pepper

3 cups water

1⅔ cups coconut milk, stirred

9 oz paneer (page 34), in 12 equal slices

MANGO AND TOMATO CURRY

⅓ cup canola oil
or ghee (page 30)

1 Tbsp black mustard seeds

1 tsp asafoetida

30 to 40 curry leaves

2 cups chopped
tomatoes (2 large)

1 tsp turmeric

1 Tbsp + 1 tsp ground cumin

1 tsp ground cayenne pepper

1 Tbsp salt

3 medium to large mangoes,
peeled, in 1-inch cubes

2 cups chopped
green onions, white
and green parts

THIS IS A seasonal curry that we serve every summer with
some variations. We sometimes use green, raw mangoes, and
our curry is more tangy than sweet. Because it's easier to buy
ripe or almost-ripe mangoes, this recipe is made with them. Be sure to
buy good-quality mangoes, though. If your mangoes have too many
strings (we refer to them as "full of moustaches"), you'll get more mango
pulp than mango flesh. Remember to cut as much flesh from the seed
as you can. If they're available, Ataulfo mangoes are the best for this dish.
Also, make sure the curry leaves you buy are green and not brownish
green. The greener the curry leaf, the more flavour it will have. If you
don't have curry leaves, you'll miss that distinct flavour but your curry
will still taste great.

Essentially, this dish is based on South Indian spicing. Fittingly, we
almost always serve this curry with chapattis, lentil chapattis (page 176)
or rice. We find that the mangoes don't taste as good with naan, and naan
is basically a north Indian bread, whereas rice and chapatti are eaten in
southern India. This curry also makes a great topping for plain, salted
crackers.

Serves 6 as an appetizer

HEAT OIL (or ghee) in a medium pot on high for 1 minute. Add mustard
seeds and cook until you hear the first popping noise. Immediately
add asafoetida and curry leaves, being careful to keep your head away
from the pan in case the water from within the curry leaves pops, and
stir. The curry leaves will shrivel as soon as you stir them in the hot oil.
Immediately reduce the heat to medium-low.

Add tomatoes, turmeric, cumin, cayenne and salt. Stir and cook
this masala for about 5 minutes. Stir in mangoes, increase the heat to
medium, cover and cook for 10 minutes, stirring halfway through. Stir in
green onions and cook, uncovered, for 2 to 3 minutes.

TO SERVE If serving as hors d'oeuvres, scoop lukewarm mango curry
into glass or ceramic bowls. Arrange crackers on a serving plate and serve
together. As a vegetarian meal with chapatti, serve the curry piping hot.

WINE An Ehrenfelser will be a great accompaniment to the sweetness
and acidity of this curry.

CURRIED BRUSSELS SPROUTS

WITH PANEER AND BACON

PANEER IS A great accompaniment to bitter vegetables such as bitter melons, rapini and Brussels sprouts. The paneer mellows the bitterness of the vegetables, and the vegetables bring out the mild flavour of the cheese. Be careful not to overcook the Brussels sprouts, or they will lose their flavour and their texture.

Do not use regular breakfast bacon for this dish. It becomes too thin and crunchy and sticks to your teeth after it's mixed with the curry. Instead, buy a thicker, meatier cut of side bacon or gammon bacon. We use about 2 ounces of bacon per person, but you can use more or less. The same goes for the paneer: we use 1 ounce per serving, but you can use more or less, according to your preference. Remember that if you use lots more of both, your dish may lose some of its spiciness. Serve this recipe as an appetizer or a light meal.

Serves 6

1½ lbs Brussels sprouts

12 oz bacon (12 thick strips)

½ cup canola oil

1½ Tbsp cumin seeds

3 cups puréed tomatoes (6 large)

1 Tbsp salt

1 tsp turmeric

1 Tbsp ground cumin

1 Tbsp ground coriander

½ tsp ground cayenne pepper

4 cups water

6 oz paneer (page 34), in 2-inch cubes

LINE A PLATE with paper towels.

Wash Brussels sprouts and cut each one in quarters, lengthwise. Set aside.

Place bacon strips in a frying pan on medium-high heat. Cook for 1 to 2 minutes, or until the edges of the bacon curl slightly. Turn the strips over and cook for another 1 to 2 minutes. Both sides should be light brown and slightly crispy, but do not allow them to become dark or burned. You may need to reduce the heat slightly. Transfer cooked bacon to the plate, cool and allow fat to drain. After about 10 minutes, cut bacon in 1-inch pieces.

Heat oil in a medium shallow pan on medium-high for 1 minute. Add cumin seeds, stir and allow to sizzle for 30 seconds. Add tomatoes, salt, turmeric, cumin, coriander and cayenne. Stir well and cook for 5 to 8 minutes, or until the top glistens with oil.

Stir in Brussels sprouts and water. Bring to a boil, reduce the heat to low, cover and simmer for 5 to 8 minutes, or until Brussels sprouts are slightly soft but not mushy.

TO SERVE Divide paneer evenly among six plates. Pour the Brussels sprouts and its curry over the paneer while it's piping hot. Sprinkle the bacon pieces over the Brussels sprouts. (Each serving should have the equivalent of 2 strips of bacon.)

WINE Brussels sprouts, paneer and bacon are a perfect match for a light red wine from the Douro region of Portugal. We recommend that you start drinking the wine while the Brussels sprouts are cooking!

SAUTÉED BRUSSELS SPROUTS

RED BELL PEPPERS, PANEER AND CASHEWS

11 oz Brussels sprouts

⅔ cup raw whole
unsalted cashews

½ cup canola oil

1 tsp black mustard seeds

¾ tsp asafoetida

1 Tbsp cumin seeds

1 tsp turmeric

2½ tsp salt

½ tsp ground
cayenne pepper

1 cup finely chopped
tomatoes (about 1 large)

1 lb paneer (page 34),
in ½-inch cubes

1 large red bell pepper,
in ½-inch cubes

¾ cup finely
chopped cilantro

W E HAVE HAD scores of customers tell us that although they don't like Brussels sprouts, they love this dish. You don't taste any of the bitterness of boiled or steamed Brussels sprouts. Vikram actually doesn't even like Brussels sprouts, unless they are cooked Indian-style and served with chapattis or rice. If you don't have a full pound of paneer, that's okay—just be sure to add extra vegetables or cashews.

Since you will use high heat, the seeds will cook very quickly in oil. Therefore, have all your ingredients ready to add to the spices immediately. *Serves 6 to 8*

CUT THE STALKS off Brussels sprouts and peel off any outer leaves that are tough or damaged. Discard these. Wash Brussels sprouts and cut each one in quarters, lengthwise. Some leaves will fall off, but be sure to keep them for cooking.

Preheat the oven or toaster oven to 375°F. Spread cashews on a baking tray and bake for 3 minutes. Gently stir cashews to roast them evenly. Return to the oven for another 3 minutes, or until golden brown. Watch carefully because cashews can burn quickly. Remove from the oven and cool for at least 30 minutes.

In a large shallow pan, heat oil for 1 minute on medium-high heat. Sprinkle in mustard seeds and allow them to sizzle until you hear the very first popping sound, about 1 minute. Quickly add asafoetida and cumin seeds and allow them to sizzle for 30 seconds. Add turmeric, salt and cayenne, reduce the heat to medium and stir for 1 minute. Be careful not to burn the seeds. (If the masala is about to burn before the 1 minute is up, turn off the heat and quickly add tomatoes and Brussels sprouts. Then return the heat to medium.)

Add tomatoes and Brussels sprouts and stir well. Cover and cook vegetables for 5 minutes. Stir in paneer and cook for another 2 minutes, uncovered. Add bell peppers and cook 2 to 3 minutes more, until vegetables are cooked but not mushy.

Just before serving, use your hands to break cashews in pieces. Stir cashew pieces and cilantro into the curry.

TO SERVE Serve piping hot in shallow ceramic bowls.

WINE Pour glasses of Moscato d'Asti and sip this wine while the Brussels sprouts are cooking, then continue drinking it when you sit down to eat.

PORTOBELLO MUSHROOMS

PORCINI CREAM CURRY

2½ Tbsp dried
porcini mushrooms

1 cup very hot water

3 Tbsp canola or olive oil

1 medium onion,
finely chopped

2½ Tbsp all-purpose flour

1 ½ cups water

½ cup whipping cream

½ tsp salt

¼ tsp ground
cayenne pepper

1½ tsp dried
fenugreek leaves

MUSHROOMS

6 large portobello
mushrooms, washed,
dried and de-stemmed

4 Tbsp canola oil

¼ tsp asafoetida

1 Tbsp garam masala
(page 26)

1 Tbsp mango powder

¼ tsp ground
cayenne pepper

2 tsp salt

 THE GARAM MASALA gives this dish its spiciness (not heat), so be sure either to make the garam masala in this cookbook or to buy a high-quality one that is darker brown in colour. Also, check the ingredients if you purchase a garam masala; try to buy one that doesn't list ground coriander. The coriander doesn't go well with the mango powder when combined with the porcini cream curry.

The portobello mushrooms in this recipe can be cut or left whole, according to your preference. Be careful not to allow the mushrooms to overcook when you sauté them, as they will continue to cook when you pour the hot curry over them.

This dish tastes great with plain white rice or naan, both of which nicely soak up the flavours of the porcini cream curry. In fact, even a baguette goes very well with this dish.

Serves 6

PORCINI CREAM CURRY Place mushrooms and 1 cup of very hot water in a bowl and allow to sit for 30 minutes. Strain mushrooms, reserving the soaking water in a small bowl. Finely chop the soaked mushrooms and set aside.

Heat oil in a medium pot on medium heat and sauté onions for 5 to 8 minutes, until brown. Stir in flour and cook for 2 to 3 minutes, until light brown. Stir in mushrooms and their soaking water, 1½ cups water, cream, salt and cayenne. Bring to a low boil and cook, uncovered, for about 15 minutes. Add fenugreek leaves, stir well and cook for another 5 minutes.

MUSHROOMS Cut each mushroom in 5 or 6 slices or, if you prefer, leave them whole.

Heat about 4 Tbsp oil (enough to cover the bottom) in a large frying pan on medium heat. Sprinkle asafoetida into the hot oil and allow it to sizzle for 30 seconds. Immediately add garam masala, mango powder, cayenne and salt and stir for 1 to 2 minutes. The spices will foam lightly. Add mushrooms and sauté, stirring regularly, for about 3 minutes. If you have left the mushrooms whole, cook them a minute or two longer.

TO SERVE Divide the warm mushrooms among plates, then top each serving with one-sixth of the hot curry sauce.

WINE A fruit-forward New World Pinot Noir is great with the mushrooms.

JALAPEÑO AND CUMIN-SPICED
PANEER AND COUSCOUS CAKES

W E'RE GIVING THIS recipe for sixteen servings instead of the regular six because it is so labour intensive. With just about the same effort, you can make twice as much and freeze leftover cakes in resealable bags for another occasion. (They can be kept frozen up to 3 months if sealed properly.)

You can eat these as snacks with chutneys as you would samosas or pakoras, or you can serve them as your starch with another vegetable zor meat dish. In this particular recipe, we find that canned crushed tomatoes taste and work better than fresh.

Serves 16

PLACE COUSCOUS in a large mixing bowl.

Heat a small frying pan on medium heat for 1 minute. Add coriander seeds and cook for 1 minute, stirring with a wooden spoon. If seeds haven't darkened, cook for another 30 seconds. Turn off the heat and cool.

Lightly pound coriander seeds in a mortar or in a bowl with a heavy spoon. (You just want to crack the seeds in half.) Add crushed coriander seeds to the couscous.

Using a hand grater, grate paneer as you would mozzarella cheese for a pizza. Add paneer to the couscous-coriander mixture, then add ricotta, salt, cumin, jalapeño peppers, garlic, tomatoes, water, egg and cilantro. Thoroughly mix, using your hands. Form about 16 cakes, each 2 inches wide by 3 inches long and about ½ inch thick.

Line a baking tray with paper towels. In a medium frying pan, heat 1 to 1½ Tbsp oil on medium-high heat. Add a little more oil, if necessary, to make sure the bottom of the pan is completely covered. Once oil has heated for 2 to 3 minutes, place 4 to 6 cakes (depending on how many can comfortably fit) in the frying pan and cook one side for 1½ minutes. Turn cakes over and cook for another 1½ minutes. Transfer cooked cakes to the tray and allow excess oil to drain. Add another 1 Tbsp oil and repeat the above steps until you have made all of the cakes.

TO SERVE If serving as an appetizer, serve warm on individual plates. If serving with a curry, arrange the cakes on individual plates then top with the curry.

WINE A South African Chenin Blanc fermented in stainless steel barrels is Vikram's pick.

1 cup cooked
couscous, cooled

1 Tbsp coriander seeds

12 oz paneer (page 34)

5 oz ricotta cheese

1 Tbsp salt

2 Tbsp ground cumin

2 Tbsp finely chopped
jalapeño peppers

2 Tbsp finely chopped garlic

2 Tbsp canned
crushed tomatoes

¾ cup water

1 egg

½ cup chopped cilantro

⅔ cup canola oil
for pan frying

SEASONAL VEGETABLES
WITH GRATED COCONUT AND BLACK CHICKPEA RICE

W E TRIED THIS recipe for the first time on a Sunday when the markets had closed for the day. At the time we were developing our new summer menu and we wanted a fresh, crispy appetizer. We had come up with the spicing we wanted to use, but didn't have any crispy vegetables in the fridge except for green and red cabbage and turnips. The intention was to use fresh summer vegetables, and that's what we wrote on the menu. After the menu was printed, however, we realized the cabbage and turnips actually tasted the best. And because it was summer, we decided to add fresh, local corn. If corn is out of season, make this dish without it—just add a little more cabbage and turnips.

Many of our customers joked about the cabbage and turnips being considered "summer" vegetables. They also joked that if we had written cabbage and turnips on the menu, they probably would never have ordered this dish. Remember, this is meant to be a crispy dish and will not taste good with overcooked vegetables. Also, make sure the rice is ready before you cook the vegetables.

The ghee is crucial to this recipe, as you need the buttery flavour to go with the kalonji seeds and lemon. Don't use butter in its place, since you need to heat it on high to sauté the spices and butter will burn. You can serve the coconut and black chickpea rice with a number of other curries, but avoid those made with lots of dairy (yogurt- or cream-based curries don't always taste good with coconut).

Serves 6

COCONUT AND BLACK CHICKPEA RICE Wash and drain black chickpeas. Soak in 2 cups of the water and ½ tsp salt overnight, or for at least 6 hours.

Drain chickpeas. Combine drained chickpeas in a medium pot with 4 cups of the water. Bring to a boil on high heat, reduce to low, cover and simmer for 40 minutes, or until cooked through. The outer skin of black chickpeas is thicker than the skin of regular yellow chickpeas, so taste one or mash one between your fingers to be sure they are fully cooked. Remove from the stove.

Soak coconut in ¾ cup warm water while you cook the rice.

Wash and drain rice in cold water at least twice. Soak rice in cold water for 15 to 20 minutes. Drain.

COCONUT AND BLACK CHICKPEA RICE

½ cup black chickpeas

6 cups water for chickpeas

½ tsp salt for chickpeas

2 Tbsp dried unsweetened shredded coconut

¾ cup warm water for coconut

1 cup basmati rice

2 cups cold water for soaking rice

2 tsp canola oil

½ tsp salt for rice

1¾ cups water for boiling rice

1 small head of
green cabbage

1 small head of
purple cabbage

1 large turnip (½ lb)

3 cups water

3 cobs of corn, husked
but uncooked

1 Tbsp cumin seeds

1 tsp kalonji seeds

2 Tbsp yellow mustard seeds

½ cup ghee (page 30)

½ cup finely chopped
tomatoes (1 small)

1 Tbsp ground coriander

1 Tbsp salt

½ tsp crushed
cayenne pepper

⅓ cup fresh lemon juice

In another medium pot, combine rice, oil, salt and the 1¾ cups water for boiling rice. Bring rice to a boil on high heat. As soon as the water is boiling vigorously, reduce the heat to low. Cover rice and cook for 15 minutes. Turn off the heat and allow to rest, without removing the lid, for another 5 minutes. Drain and discard the water from the coconut by pouring it through a sieve. Using a fork, stir coconut into the rice.

Drain chickpeas and stir them into the rice. Cover and set aside.

VEGETABLES Wash and cut green and purple cabbage into pieces about ¼ inch wide and 2 inches long. They can be a little wider, but not thinner. You want to be able to eat the cabbage with your fork, but this is not coleslaw. Set cut cabbage aside.

Cut turnip in thin circles (⅙ inch thick), then cut each circle into quarters. Set aside.

In a medium pot, bring the 3 cups of water to a vigorous boil on high heat. Using a sharp knife, shave corn kernels off the cob. Fill a bowl with very cold water. Add corn kernels to boiling water and blanch by boiling for 30 seconds. Drain immediately in a colander, then immerse corn in the cold water and soak for 1 minute to stop the cooking. Drain again once the water is no longer cold. The corn should be cooked but crispy.

Combine cumin, kalonji and mustard seeds in a small bowl. Heat ghee in a medium pot for 1 minute on high heat. Reduce the heat to medium and add the mixed seeds. Stir well and allow them to sizzle. After 1½ to 2 minutes, you will hear the first mustard seeds popping. Immediately add tomatoes and stir. Add coriander, salt and cayenne and cook for 3 to 4 minutes.

Add turnips and cook, stirring regularly, for 2 minutes. Just before serving, add cabbage and cook for another 2 to 3 minutes. Stir in corn, then stir in lemon juice.

TO SERVE Divide rice among six bowls and ladle vegetables over top. (Be sure to include the ghee with the cumin, kalonji and mustard seeds with the vegetables.)

WINE An unoaked Chardonnay from a cool climate such as British Columbia's Okanagan pairs very nicely with this dish.

POTATO AND CAULIFLOWER
PAKORAS (FRITTERS)

DESPITE THE FACT that pakoras are deep-fried, they are actually quite healthy: they are full of vegetables and chickpea flour. Known as besan in Hindi and Punjabi, chickpea flour is a versatile, delicious and satisfying ingredient for many vegetarian and vegan dishes. Its flavour is not at all bitter but is much stronger than the flavour of chapatti flour or any white flour. It is now also readily available at most non-Indian gourmet or organic grocers.

Although pakoras are mostly eaten as a snack with chutney (or ketchup!) at any time of the day, we also serve them with the Tomato, Coriander and Ginger Soup (page 45) as a vegetarian entrée.

It is hard to get a cauliflower that weighs exactly 1 pound, so we have used the average weight of a whole, large cauliflower cut in florets. Make sure that all of your vegetables are fully dried after washing them, otherwise the extra water will make the batter runny.

Store any uneaten pakoras in an airtight container or a resealable bag, either refrigerated for up to 3 days or frozen for up to 1 month. Just reheat them on a baking tray in a preheated 350°F oven for 15 minutes. Be sure to thaw the frozen pakoras before reheating them.

Serves 6

1 lb cauliflower, in 1-inch florets

10 oz russet potato (1 large)

3½ cups chickpea flour

2½ cups buttermilk

3 jalapeño peppers, finely chopped

3 Tbsp ground coriander

3 Tbsp ground cumin

1 tsp mango powder

1 tsp turmeric

2 Tbsp salt

1 red onion, sliced lengthwise

6 cups oil for deep frying

WASH CAULIFLOWER in a colander and set aside. Allow water to drain from cauliflower for 15 to 20 minutes.

Peel and wash potatoes. Cut each potato in half, and cut each half in thin slices, about ⅛ inch thick.

In a large mixing bowl, combine chickpea flour, buttermilk, jalapeño peppers, coriander, cumin, mango powder, turmeric and salt, using your hands. Make sure all the small chunks of chickpea flour have dissolved and the spices are well mixed. Add cauliflower, potatoes and onions, and stir well. The vegetables and chickpea batter should stick together.

To make sure you have the right consistency, form a 2-inch ball of the mixture and gently drop it from an 8- to 10-inch height back into the mixing bowl. The ball should retain its shape for a few seconds. If the batter is too runny, add chickpea flour, 2 Tbsp at a time, until the mixture thickens up. Do not add more than 4 Tbsp in total.

Preheat a deep fryer to high heat or pour oil into a large heavy-bottomed pot and heat it on high heat for 5 minutes. Drop a very small piece of batter into the oil. If it floats to the top within a few seconds and is readily sizzling, the oil is hot enough. If it sinks to the bottom, the oil isn't yet properly heated.

When the oil is ready, using a slotted spoon, drop 2-inch balls of the batter (they won't be exactly round) into the hot oil. Drop as many as you can handle at one time, but make sure they don't touch—otherwise they will stick together. Cook for 2 to 2½ minutes, or until golden brown. Take pakoras out and drain on paper towels.

TO SERVE Arrange the pakoras on a glass or ceramic serving dish and serve them while they are still hot. If you are serving them with Tomato, Coriander and Ginger Soup, divide an equal number of pakoras among six large bowls and ladle hot soup over the pakoras.

WINE Skip the wine and go for a local, unfiltered beer such as an India Pale Ale or a wheat beer.

POTATO POORIS

1 cup mashed russet potato

½ Tbsp salt

1⅔ cups all-purpose flour

2 Tbsp + ¼ tsp canola oil

½ Tbsp fennel seeds

½ Tbsp ajwain seeds

1 tsp ground black pepper

6 cups oil for deep frying

POORIS ARE DEEP-FRIED unleavened breads. At Vij's, we serve these potato pooris as a snack to our customers while they are waiting for a table. We have also served them with our chicken liver pâté (page 42). They are delicious with any type of alcoholic drink, especially red wine.

Although you don't necessarily taste the potato, it is the ingredient that makes these pooris so soft on the inside. If you wish to serve these pooris as the main bread with your meal, roll out the batter to any size you choose.

Makes thirty 2½-inch pooris

LINE A BAKING tray with waxed paper. Combine mashed potatoes, salt and 1 cup of the flour in a large mixing bowl. Set aside.

Heat 2 Tbsp of the oil on medium heat in a small frying pan for 1 minute. Add fennel and ajwain seeds and allow to sizzle for 30 seconds (do not let them burn). Remove from the heat and cool for about 10 minutes.

Add cooled seeds and oil to the potato mixture. Wearing latex gloves, knead the dough until it is well mixed, all the clumps are gone and the dough is firm enough to use with a rolling pin. Rub the remaining ¼ tsp of the oil between your hands, then roll the dough around in your hands to lightly cover it with this oil. This will make the dough easier to roll out and it won't stick to the rolling pin. Set aside a ¼-inch ball of dough.

Pour the remaining ⅔ cup flour onto a flat plate.

Form dough in 1-inch balls. Roll each ball in flour, then, using a rolling pin, form it in a circle ⅛ inch thick and 2½ inches in diameter. You should have about 30 pooris. Place pooris in single rows on the baking tray. If there is not enough space for all the pooris in one layer, set another sheet of waxed paper on top of the potato breads and add another layer of pooris on top of that.

Line a metal colander with paper towels. Preheat a deep fryer to high heat or pour oil into a large heavy-bottomed pot and heat it on high heat for 5 minutes. Drop the ¼-inch ball of dough into the oil. If it floats to the top within a few seconds and is readily sizzling, the oil is hot enough. If it sinks to the bottom, the oil isn't yet properly heated. When the oil is ready, using a slotted spoon, place a few pooris at a time in the hot oil. Fry each poori for about 45 seconds on each side, or until both sides are golden brown. Remove pooris from the oil and transfer to the colander to drain. (Replace the paper towels if they become too greasy.)

TO SERVE Arrange pooris in a napkin-lined serving bowl or on a glass platter. Serve hot.

WINE These pooris are delicious with various wines, red or white. Choose your favourite.

PRAWNS IN COCONUT MASALA

THIS RECIPE CAN be served as an appetizer or passed around with drinks. On its own, the masala goes well with naan or rice. You can substitute canola oil for the ghee in this recipe but remember that you will lose some flavour. Don't substitute butter. It is difficult to cook cumin seeds alone in butter, as you need to keep the heat relatively high and the butter ends up burning and sticking to the bottom of your pot. Also, use a good-quality coconut milk. You don't use very much but you want to be able to taste it in your recipe. Adding a larger quantity of a low-quality coconut milk just makes this dish runny.

If we can't source any wild prawns, we use prawns farmed in the U.S., specifically California, rather than Asian-farmed tiger prawns. The farming practices of many tiger prawn farms in Asia are considered highly questionable by organizations monitoring healthy and/or sustainable seafoods. Prawns cook very quickly—2 to 3 minutes on average—so watch them closely to avoid overcooking them.

Serves 6

30 prawns,
shelled and deveined

2 tsp salt

2 Tbsp ghee (page 30)
or canola oil

½ Tbsp cumin seeds

2 large onions, chopped

3 large ripe tomatoes,
finely chopped

2 Tbsp coconut milk, stirred

2 Tbsp red wine vinegar

2 tsp chopped green chilies

3 bunches green onions,
white and green parts,
chopped

PLACE PRAWNS in a colander and rinse under cold water. Allow excess water to drain. In a bowl, combine prawns and 1 tsp of the salt. Cover with plastic wrap and set aside in the refrigerator while you are making the coconut masala.

In a large frying pan, melt ghee on medium-high heat (or heat oil for 1 minute). Add cumin seeds and allow them to sizzle for 30 seconds. Add onions and sauté 5 to 8 minutes, or until dark brown but not burned. Stir in tomatoes, coconut milk, vinegar, chilies and the remaining 1 tsp of salt. Cook for 5 minutes, or until tomatoes are cooked through. Add green onions and stir well.

Add prawns, stirring constantly until they become pinkish-orange. This will take about 3 minutes. Immediately remove from the heat.

TO SERVE Place 5 prawns on each of six small shallow plates. Top each serving with one-sixth of the coconut masala. Alternatively, divide the coconut masala evenly among six small shallow plates, then top with 5 prawns per plate.

WINE A Pouilly-Fumé or Sancerre wine is a great sipping wine with this masala.

BEEF KEBOBS

WITH CREAMY BENGALI-STYLE CURRY

 THIS RECIPE COMES from Anjum Sultana, one of our cooks, who is originally from Pakistan. This is a popular recipe and is easy as well as delicious. Anjum steams these kebobs in a covered pan instead of grilling them. Although we were initially dubious (Mike, our manager, insisted that we shouldn't write "steamed" on the menu, fearing that customers wouldn't order them), Anjum was right: these kebobs are very popular with our customers. In Pakistan, ground lamb or goat is often used instead of beef.

We recommend that you use lean ground beef, but not the extra lean. A little bit of fat makes tender kebobs. It is also important that you steam the kebobs in a pan small enough that the uncooked kebobs can be stacked in at least two tight rows. If your pan is too large, not enough steam will be produced and the kebobs on the bottom of the pan will burn.

We serve these kebobs with our Creamy Bengali-style Curry, which also tastes great on its own over a bowl of rice, or with our Panfried Salmon Potato Cakes (page 122). You can even serve this curry sauce over any grilled red meat—for example, lamb or beef tenderloin—without adding any additional spices to the meat. Naan, or even a fresh baguette, will soak up the cream and panch poran flavours very nicely.

You can also serve just the kebobs as appetizers, with any type of chutney.

Makes 25 to 30 kebobs

BEEF KEBOBS In a large mixing bowl, combine all ingredients with your hands until thoroughly mixed. Form in slightly elongated mini–hot dog shapes, each 2 inches × 1 inch.

Place kebobs in a medium heavy-bottomed pot, spacing them so they completely cover the bottom. The kebobs should be loosely touching each other. Place a second layer of kebobs on top of the first. Once you have placed all kebobs in the pot, cover with a tight-fitting lid and turn on the heat to medium. Cook for about 20 minutes, checking about halfway through to make sure the steam has released enough water and fat at the bottom of the pot to cook the kebobs. If they are burning, reduce the heat to medium-low or transfer the kebobs to a smaller pot. To check if kebobs are done, insert a knife into the middle of the meat. If meat is only very slightly pink or not pink at all, kebobs are done.

CREAM CURRY Heat oil in a medium pot on medium-high heat for 30 seconds. Add panch poran and allow to sizzle for 30 seconds. It should foam slightly. Immediately add tomatoes and stir, so spices do not burn. Stir in salt, turmeric and cayenne. Cook for 5 to 8 minutes, or until oil glistens on top.

Stir in water, cover the pot and bring to a boil. Stir well, reduce the heat to low and simmer, covered, for 15 minutes. Add cream, stir and continue simmering, covered, for another 5 minutes.

TO SERVE Place 4 to 5 kebobs in each bowl. Pour 1 cup of piping hot curry over each serving.

WINE A young Beaujolais will balance the intensity of the flavours in this dish.

BEEF KEBOBS

1½ lbs lean ground beef

8 oz onion, finely chopped (1 medium to large)

3 Tbsp chopped ginger

1 tsp ground cayenne pepper

4 Tbsp ground or finely chopped jalapeño peppers

1½ Tbsp garam masala (page 26)

1 cup finely chopped cilantro

1 Tbsp salt

CREAM CURRY

⅓ cup canola oil

3 Tbsp ground panch poran (page 28)

3 cups puréed fresh tomatoes (6 large)

1 Tbsp salt

½ tsp turmeric

½ Tbsp crushed cayenne pepper

5½ cups water

1 cup whipping cream

GRILLED LAMB OR MUTTON KEBOBS

1 egg

1 Tbsp canola oil

1 cup puréed onions (1 large)

2 lbs ground lamb
or mutton

3 Tbsp finely chopped ginger

3 Tbsp finely chopped garlic

1½ Tbsp finely chopped
jalapeño peppers

½ Tbsp salt

2 Tbsp paprika

1 tsp crushed
cayenne pepper

twenty-four 12-inch
metal skewers

THIS IS A staple appetizer at Vij's, even though it could just as easily be a main course. We always serve these kebobs with a salad such as the Beet and Daikon Salsa (page 157) or with organic greens tossed with some oil and vinegar. As well, we serve them with Mint Mango Chutney (page 159) and with Date Chutney (page 158).

If you don't chop the ginger, garlic and jalapeño peppers fine enough, the bigger pieces could break the kebobs while you are grilling them. Do not buy extra lean ground meat because you need some fat in the meat for grilling and to make them juicy. You can make these kebobs ahead of time and refrigerate them up to 1 day before grilling them.

Serves 6

BEAT EGG in a small bowl and reserve half of it for this recipe.

Place oil in a small, heavy frying pan on medium heat. Add onions and sauté for 8 to 10 minutes, stirring constantly, until browned. Remove from the heat and transfer to a bowl (scrape any bits of onions sticking to the pan into the bowl as well). Cool for at least 15 minutes.

In a large bowl, combine lamb (or mutton), ginger, garlic, jalapeño peppers, salt, paprika, cayenne, egg and onions. Mix well with your hands until thoroughly combined. Cover with plastic wrap and refrigerate for 30 minutes, or until meat is firm enough to shape and place onto skewers.

Preheat a barbeque or stovetop cast-iron grill to high heat (remember to turn on the stovetop fan, since cooking the meat will emit some smoke). Divide cooled meat in twelve equal parts. Wrap each part around one skewer, forming a kebob 8 or 9 inches long and 1 inch wide. Place kebobs on the grill and cook for 4 to 5 minutes, turning often. Kebobs should be well done but not charred or blackened. If they are cooking too quickly, reduce the heat slightly. Poke the meat with a knife to be sure it's completely cooked inside.

TO SERVE Using an oven glove or a cloth, hold the hot skewer with one hand, and with the other, use a fork or knife to push the cooked meat off the skewer. Place the meat from 2 skewers on each plate, with chutneys.

WINE We recommend a Cabernet Franc from the Loire Valley in France.

Meat

Ground Beef Curry with
Warm Fennel and Zucchini Salad 70

Demerara Sugar and Tamarind-marinated
Beef Tenderloin with Black Cumin Curry 73

Beef Short Ribs in Cinnamon and Red-wine Curry 75

Seared Venison Medallions with Fig and Roasted
Pomegranate Khoa in a Pomegranate Curry 76

Stewed Cinnamon-scented Goat or Lamb Curry 80

Coriander and Black Cardamom
Lamb in Buttermilk Curry 81

Marinated Lamb Popsicles
with Fenugreek Cream Curry 83

Oven-braised Goat Meat in
Fennel and Kalonji Curry 84

Spice-encrusted Pork 86

Pork Tenderloin with Spinach and Fig Stew 88

GROUND BEEF CURRY

WITH WARM FENNEL AND ZUCCHINI SALAD

GROUND BEEF CURRY

½ cup canola oil

2 cups puréed
onions (2 large)

1½ cups puréed tomatoes
(2 large plus 1 medium)

1½ Tbsp ground cumin

1 Tbsp + 1 tsp salt

1 tsp turmeric

½ Tbsp ground
cayenne pepper

1 cup whipping cream

1 lb 10 oz extra lean
or lean ground beef

3 oz raw sugar (½ cup
chopped and packed)

1½ tsp dried mint (optional)

 GROUND MEAT CURRY is known as *keema* in Hindi. In India, it is usually made from goat, mutton or lamb. We recommend that you use extra lean ground beef. Since you cook the meat in the masala, you can't drain any excess fat from the meat without draining all the spices as well.

On its own, this is a pretty rich curry, which is why we serve the warm fennel and zucchini salad to balance it. Try to find the smaller, organic zucchini. They are much sweeter than the large, regular ones, which sometimes taste like bitter paper.

This recipe needs very little preparation. It does, however, require a few special ingredients. The dried mint is optional, but if you can get some, it's worth including. You can buy raw sugar from any Indian grocer. It is usually sold in hard chunks, which you can cut and mash with a good knife. If you can't cut and mash it, just cut it in the smallest chunks you can. This dish tastes great with naan and with raita (page 156) on the side.

Serves 6 to 8

GROUND BEEF CURRY Heat oil in a medium heavy-bottomed frying pan on medium-high heat for 1 minute. Add onions and sauté, stirring regularly, for 15 minutes, or until brown. (It takes longer for puréed onions to brown than chopped onions, and the puréed onions will stick a little to the bottom of the pan.) Add tomatoes, cumin, salt, turmeric and cayenne and sauté for another 5 minutes, or until oil glistens.

Add cream, stir well and cook for another 4 to 5 minutes. Break up ground beef and add it to the curry. Stir well so you don't get big chunks of ground beef in the curry. Cook for 6 minutes, then check to make sure the beef is cooked to your liking. If not, cook for another couple of minutes and check again. If the beef overcooks, it will harden and lose its tenderness.

Stir in raw sugar and mint, and cook until sugar melts into beef (about 1 minute if sugar is already chopped, longer if the chunks are larger). Turn off the heat as soon as sugar melts. Cool for 5 minutes, cover with a lid and set aside while you prepare the salad.

WARM FENNEL AND ZUCCHINI SALAD Heat oil in a nonstick frying pan on medium-high heat for 30 seconds. Add garlic and sauté for 3 to 4 minutes, or until light golden. Stir in salt and turmeric and cook for 1 minute. The garlic will cook a little more as well and will look darker. Add jalapeño peppers, tomatoes and fennel. Cook and stir for 3 minutes.

Just before serving, add zucchini and cook for 2 minutes. The zucchini and fennel should be slightly crunchy. Turn off the heat and stir in lemon juice.

TO SERVE Divide warm ground beef curry among six to eight bowls. Serve warm salad over the curry.

WINE Choose a Chianti DOC (Denomination Origine Controlata) with a slight acidity.

WARM FENNEL AND ZUCCHINI SALAD

¼ cup canola oil

2 Tbsp finely chopped garlic

2 tsp salt

½ tsp turmeric

1 Tbsp chopped jalapeño peppers

1 cup chopped tomatoes (1 large)

9 oz fennel bulbs, in ¼- to ½-inch sticks

10 oz zucchini, in 2-inch sticks

½ Tbsp lemon juice

DEMERARA SUGAR AND TAMARIND-MARINATED

BEEF TENDERLOIN

WITH BLACK CUMIN CURRY

B EFORE VIKRAM LEFT Mumbai for hotel management school in Austria, the only meats he had ever eaten were goat and chicken, both of them thoroughly stewed in curries. He had never touched beef or pork, so when he arrived in Austria and was presented with a plate of beef tongue, he just couldn't eat it. Student dinners usually consisted of either beef or pork, which Vikram politely declined. His mother had packed him a big jar of Indian pickles, and after dinner he would go back to the dorm room and eat the pickles with plain bread. After a month, however, the pickles ran out and Vikram decided he would have to try beef. It was love at first bite—only now, the rarer the better.

Traditionally, Indians eat thoroughly cooked meats and avoid rare or medium-rare red meat. So, a note to those who eat only well-done red meats: a well-done beef tenderloin will be chewy and really isn't worth the money you'll spend.

The key to this recipe is balance between the demerara sugar and the tamarind. After you mix the ingredients but before you add the tenderloin steaks, dip your finger in the mixture and taste it. Depending on whether you make your tamarind paste (page 32) or buy it, its tartness will vary. And, since sweet and tart are very personal preferences, add more sugar or tamarind paste if you so wish.

These steaks are delicious on their own with a traditional baked potato or side salad. The curry can also be eaten on its own as a soup, with rice or poured over many red meats, poultry, fish or vegetables. At Vij's, we make black cumin curry as a gravy for the steaks and serve them with salad and basmati rice.

Make sure that you roast the cumin seeds (page 29) yourself and get them as dark brown as possible without actually burning them. Since it is difficult to roast just 1 tablespoon of cumin seeds evenly without burning them, we suggest that you heat 2 tablespoons and reserve the remaining seeds for another use. Once the dark cumin mixes into the curry, it appears black. Although we also use ground cumin, the roasted flavour of the blackened cumin seeds is predominant here.

Serves 6

BEEF TENDERLOIN

5 oz demerara sugar

⅔ cup tamarind paste (page 32)

3½ Tbsp ground coriander

1 Tbsp ground cayenne pepper

½ Tbsp salt

⅓ cup canola or olive oil

6 beef tenderloin steaks, each 5 oz

....

CHICKEN STOCK

1 lb chicken bones

11 cups water

1 onion, roughly chopped

2 or 3 small carrots with greens, roughly chopped

1 Tbsp salt

½ tsp ground black pepper

....

BLACK CUMIN SEEDS

2 Tbsp cumin seeds

....

BLACK CUMIN CURRY

½ cup ghee (page 30)

2½ cups finely chopped onions (2 medium to large)

1 Tbsp roasted black cumin seeds

½ cup all-purpose flour

1 Tbsp salt

½ tsp ground cayenne pepper

1 Tbsp ground cumin

1 Tbsp ground coriander

1 cup finely chopped tomatoes (1 large)

5 cups chicken stock

1 cup water

BEEF TENDERLOIN Combine sugar, tamarind, coriander, cayenne, salt and oil in a large mixing bowl. Poke each tenderloin steak 5 or 6 times with a knife (this helps the marinade to soak into the meat), then mix steaks into the sugar-tamarind mixture. Make sure steaks are well covered in the marinade. Cover the bowl with plastic wrap and refrigerate for at least 3 hours.

CHICKEN STOCK Combine chicken bones, water, onions, carrots and greens, salt and pepper in a large pot with a lid. Bring to a boil on medium heat. Reduce the heat to low, cover and simmer for 2 hours. Check that there is enough water in the pot to keep the bones and vegetables covered at all times. Turn off the heat and allow the stock to cool.

Place a fine-mesh sieve over another pot or a stainless steel bowl. Using a ladle, strain chicken stock into the pot (or bowl) and discard solids. You should have about 5 cups of stock. Set aside. (Will keep in the refrigerator for 3 to 4 days, or frozen for up to 1 month, in a sealed container.)

BLACK CUMIN SEEDS Heat a small frying pan on medium heat for 1 minute. Add cumin seeds and heat them, stirring constantly, for 2 to 3 minutes or until dark brown. Transfer darkened seeds to a bowl and set aside to cool.

BLACK CUMIN CURRY Melt ghee in a medium pot on medium heat. Add onions and cumin seeds and stir. (The cumin seeds don't need to sizzle or cook in the oil first, since they were roasted to dark brown.) Sauté onions for 10 minutes, then add flour, stir well and reduce the heat to low. Stirring regularly, cook flour for 6 to 7 minutes. The flour will darken. Add salt, cayenne, ground cumin, coriander and tomatoes, stir well and cook for 5 minutes. The masala will be quite doughy.

Add chicken stock and water and increase the heat to medium. Stir well. Bring to a boil, uncovered, then turn off the heat.

FINISH TENDERLOIN Preheat a grill, barbeque or stovetop cast-iron grill to high heat. Grill marinated steaks on one side for about 2 minutes and then turn over. Grill the other side for 2 minutes. This is a fairly rare steak. If you prefer your steak cooked medium-rare, return to the grill for 1 to 2 minutes on each side.

TO SERVE Arrange 1 steak on each plate. Ladle curry over each serving.

WINE Drink a big fruit-forward California Cabernet Sauvignon.

BEEF SHORT RIBS
IN CINNAMON AND RED-WINE CURRY

THIS IS A rich curry, so enjoy it and don't be stingy with the ghee. If you don't have any ghee, you can substitute butter, but remember that butter burns at a high heat. You don't have to melt the ghee before measuring it for the recipe. If at any time the onions or tomato masala begin to stick to the bottom of the pan or look as though they're about to burn, either lower the heat or add 1 Tbsp of canola oil or ghee. Do not add water. Remember, this is meant to be a rich curry with lots of onions and garlic.

Smell the cinnamon bark. If it's very strong smelling, break the bark in half and only use one half. If the whole piece is not strong enough, add an extra half bark. Smell for the cinnamon throughout the cooking process. You should smell a mild cinnamon flavour instead of a strong one. If cinnamon is the only spice you smell, take out the bark and continue cooking the curry without it. Serve this curry with naan and/or rice. Or, serve with hot Cassava Fries (page 164).

Serves 6 to 8

IN A LARGE, heavy pot with a tight-fitting lid, melt ghee on medium to high heat. (If using butter, melt on low heat and increase the heat to medium after adding the cooking oil.) Add oil and cumin seeds. Allow seeds to sizzle for 30 seconds, then add onions. Sauté onions 8 to 10 minutes, or until brown. Add garlic and sauté until garlic is golden brown and onions are a darker brown, about 3 minutes. The darker you sauté the onions without letting them burn, the richer the onion flavour will be in this curry.

Reduce the heat to low and add tomatoes, fenugreek, cumin, turmeric, cayenne, chili and cinnamon bark. Stir well, then increase the heat to medium. Cook, stirring regularly, until ghee/oil separates from the tomatoes, about 10 minutes. Stir in stock and red wine and bring to a boil. Cover and simmer, stirring occasionally, for about 15 minutes, or until ghee/oil separates from the stock and rises to the top.

Add short ribs and stir well. Bring to a boil, cover and simmer for about 4 hours, stirring occasionally.

TO SERVE Place 1 short rib in each bowl. Ladle curry equally among the bowls, pouring it over the short ribs.

WINE An Australian Shiraz from the McLaren Vale region nicely balances the cinnamon and red-wine curry.

2 Tbsp ghee
(page 30) or butter

¼ cup canola oil

1 Tbsp cumin seeds

1 lb onions, finely chopped
(2 large)

10 cloves garlic,
finely chopped

1 cup puréed fresh tomatoes
(2 large)

1 tsp ground fenugreek seeds

1½ Tbsp ground cumin

½ tsp turmeric

½ tsp ground
cayenne pepper

1½ Tbsp Mexican
chili powder

1 whole piece cinnamon
bark (about 3 inches long)

5 cups vegetable or chicken
stock, fat skimmed off

½ cup red wine

2½ lbs beef short ribs,
bone removed and excess
fat trimmed (each rib
about 7 oz raw)

SEARED VENISON MEDALLIONS

WITH FIG AND ROASTED POMEGRANATE KHOA

IN A POMEGRANATE CURRY

THIS IS PROBABLY one of the most complicated recipes in this book, even without making the khoa. Nevertheless, if you have made some of the other dishes in this book, we suggest that you take a couple of hours and try this one as well for a very uniquely flavoured meat dish.

The most important fruit and spice here is the pomegranate. We use regular dried pomegranate seeds in the stock for a tart flavour. In the marinade, we use roasted and ground pomegranate seeds for a slightly earthy and sweet flavour. (If you use your coffee grinder to grind the seeds, don't worry about smelling it up. You just need to wipe your grinder with a paper towel.) You can buy the pomegranate seeds at any Indian grocer, and they are also known as *anardana* in Hindi. You will note that although they are referred to as "dried" pomegranate seeds, they are nevertheless quite moist and sticky.

We use the boneless Denver leg cut of the meat. We marinate the venison in oil and the ground pomegranate seeds and make a separate pomegranate curry from the regular seeds. The curry may seem a little too tart on its own, but it is perfect with the venison and the khoa.

At Vij's we make our own khoa. As cherished in India as ghee, real khoa is even more expensive and harder to come by. Basically, it is whole milk that is as condensed as milk can possibly get. It is sometimes referred to as milk fudge. At Vij's we place the milk in a large, heavy Indian wok called a *karai*. As the milk solidifies along the edges of the karai, we scrape it back into the pot. We do this for about three hours, until all the milk has solidified and been scraped off the sides. The entire process is very labour intensive and tedious, but we all love khoa.

When we first started making khoa at Vij's, there were many complaints as to whose turn it was to make it. This task became on par with dishwashing. However, because we were all so excited about having real khoa in the kitchen, many of us were sneaking 1 to 2 tablespoons' worth every day, melting it in the microwave and adding a teaspoon of sugar. Some were probably taking more, and the proof was in our simultaneous weight gain. That took care of khoa abuse in our kitchen.

We use khoa in small quantities as a creamy, rich accent to our meat dishes, though in India it is usually used to make desserts, most importantly the different barfis—the pink, green and white squares you see in the dessert section of Indian restaurants. Khoa is also used in many of our halwas, including our carrot and squash versions. Remember that if the dessert is cheap, there's not much real khoa in it.

POMEGRANATE SEEDS

½ cup dried
pomegranate seed

....

VENISON

1 cup canola oil

1 tsp salt

½ tsp ground black pepper

1 Tbsp ground roasted
pomegranate seeds

2¼ lbs boneless venison
Denver (hind) leg

Many Indians substitute ricotta cheese for khoa, and we also make that recommendation if you can't buy it. If you use ricotta, choose the whole milk variety. Although the khoa looks prettier and tastes smoother, the taste difference between the two is not that far apart.

Serve this dish with turmeric new potatoes (page 166), rice or naan.
Serves 6

....

POMEGRANATE SEEDS Before you begin, squeeze a handful of the dried pomegranate seeds in one hand and take note of how moist and sticky they are. This will help you gauge later if they have roasted enough.

In a small frying pan, heat pomegranate seeds on low heat, stirring regularly, for 10 minutes. Remove from the heat and cool for 5 to 10 minutes, then spread them out on a flat plate or a baking tray. Cool for another 10 minutes.

Squeeze a handful of the seeds to make sure they feel much drier than they did before you roasted them. They should no longer stick to your hand and they should fall off with a flick of your hand. If they don't feel drier, cook them for another 5 minutes on low heat.

Grind seeds, in small batches if necessary, in a coffee or spice grinder. Do not grind them for long because the seeds can stick to the grinder and burn out the motor. Depending on how dry the seeds were, you will either get a lot or a little bit of ground pomegranate powder. Empty ground seeds and powder into a fine-mesh sieve and sift into a bowl. Discard the seeds that didn't grind. Measure 1 Tbsp + 1 tsp of the ground powder and set aside. The remaining powder will keep in a cool, dry place for up to 3 months in a sealed container.

VENISON In a large mixing bowl, combine oil, salt, black pepper and ground pomegranate seeds. Set the marinade aside.

Cut venison leg lengthwise along the grain in 3 long pieces. Cut each of these 3 long pieces in eight 1½-oz cubes, each about 2½ to 3 inches. With a mallet, gently pound each of the 24 pieces of venison 4 to 5 times. Each piece should flatten a little, forming a "medallion."

Mix venison in the marinade, making sure to coat the pieces well. Cover the bowl with plastic wrap and refrigerate for at least 6 hours or up to 2 days. The longer the venison marinates, the stronger all of the flavours will be.

POMEGRANATE CURRY Lightly pound black cardamoms and peel off the skin. Empty the moist seeds into a large pot. Discard the skins. Add pomegranate seeds, sugar and water and bring to a boil on high heat. Reduce the heat, cover and simmer for 35 to 40 minutes. Turn off the heat and cool for at least 30 minutes.

Set a large fine-mesh sieve over another pot. Using a large ladle, strain the cardamom-pomegranate mixture through the sieve. Discard pomegranate and black cardamom seeds. Set this stock aside.

Heat ghee in a medium pot on medium heat. As soon as it has melted, add cumin seeds and allow them to sizzle for 45 seconds. Add onions and sauté for 8 to 10 minutes, until brown. Stir in flour and cook, stirring regularly, for another 6 to 7 minutes, until light brown. Stir in cumin, cayenne and salt and cook for 1 minute, stirring regularly. Pour in pomegranate stock and stir well. Reduce the heat to low and simmer curry, uncovered, for 15 minutes. Be sure to stir regularly. Remove from the heat, cover and set aside.

FIG AND KHOA FILLING In a small frying pan, sauté onions in oil on medium heat for 4 to 5 minutes. Reduce the heat to low and add figs. Sauté for another 2 minutes. Add khoa (or ricotta cheese) and cook until it melts completely, in 2 to 3 minutes (or 10 minutes for the ricotta cheese, stirring constantly). Add ground pomegranate, salt and cayenne and cook for 1 minute. Turn off the heat, cool for 5 minutes and transfer to a bowl.

FINISH VENISON Heat a frying pan on medium heat for 2 minutes. Mix marinated venison once more to make sure oil and spices are thoroughly coating the meat. Place 4 pieces of venison in the frying pan and sear one side for about 2 minutes. Turn venison over and sear for another 2 minutes, for medium rare. As soon as the venison is cooked, place two medallions side by side on a plate and top each one with ¾ to 1 tsp of the fig-khoa filling. Cover each with another medallion.

Cook the remaining venison, assembling ten more stacks of meat layered with the fig-khoa mixture.

TO SERVE Just before serving, heat the pomegranate curry on medium heat until it comes to a boil. Reduce the heat to low. Arrange 2 stacks of medallions on each plate. Pour piping hot pomegranate curry over the venison.

WINE A Bordeaux AOC (Appellation d'Origine Controlée) is perfect with the gamey flavour of the venison.

POMEGRANATE CURRY

8 black cardamom pods

9 oz ground dried pomegranate seeds

2 Tbsp white sugar

10 cups water

¾ cup ghee (page 30)

1 Tbsp cumin seeds

1 lb onions, finely chopped

½ cup all-purpose flour

1 Tbsp ground cumin

1 tsp ground cayenne pepper

1 Tbsp salt

FIG AND KHOA FILLING

1 cup finely chopped onions (1 large)

2 Tbsp + 1 tsp canola oil

2½ oz dried figs, finely chopped (about 8 figs)

1 cup khoa (or ricotta cheese)

1 tsp ground roasted pomegranate seeds

1 tsp salt

¼ tsp ground cayenne pepper

GOAT OR LAMB CURRY

4 to 5 Tbsp ghee (page 30)
or canola oil

1 Tbsp cumin seeds

2 large onions, chopped

7 large cloves garlic,
chopped (about 1 oz)

1 Tbsp finely chopped or
lightly crushed ginger

2 Tbsp ground cumin

2 tsp ground coriander

1 tsp turmeric

10 cloves

1 cinnamon stick,
2 inches long (add another
1-inch stick if you prefer
a stronger taste)

1 tsp ground cayenne pepper

2 Tbsp salt

5 ripe tomatoes, chopped
(about 1½ lbs)

1 cup plain yogurt, stirred

1 cup water

¼ cup canola oil

2 lbs leg of lamb
or goat, fat trimmed,
cut in 1½-inch cubes

½ cup chopped
fresh cilantro

 HIS IS VIKRAM'S favourite recipe for a stewed meat curry. In India, we use goat meat, as it is the most popular red meat there. Lamb works just as well, so choose the meat you prefer. You can buy goat meat from many Indian or Middle Eastern grocers. If you are cooking with goat, make sure you buy the leg meat, as this cut makes the best stew.

The curry tastes much richer and better if you use the ghee. If you don't have any ghee, use canola oil instead. Serve this home-style curry with chapattis or rice.

Serves 6

MELT GHEE (or 4 Tbsp of oil) on medium heat in a large, heavy stock-pot. Add cumin seeds and sauté until they sizzle, about 45 seconds. Add onions and sauté until golden brown, about 8 to 10 minutes. Add garlic and sauté 2 to 3 minutes, or until golden brown. Stir in ginger. After 1 minute, add ground cumin, coriander, turmeric, cloves, cinnamon, cayenne and salt. Cook on medium heat, stirring regularly, for 5 to 10 minutes or until ghee (or oil) separates from the spices. Add another table-spoon of ghee or oil if spices are sticking to the bottom of the pot.

Add tomatoes and cook for 3 to 4 minutes, until ghee (or oil) separates again and glistens. Stir in yogurt and cook for another 1 to 2 minutes, then add water (add an extra cup of water if serving with rice). Bring to a boil, then remove from the heat.

In another large, heavy frying pan, add ¼ cup oil (make sure there is enough to lightly cover the bottom of the pan). On medium to high heat, sauté lamb (or goat), stirring regularly, until you notice small, thin lines of blood on the meat. Remove from the heat and transfer meat to the stew.

Return stew to medium-low heat and cook covered, stirring occasion-ally, for 2 hours or until meat is cooked through. Add more water, ½ cup at a time, if the stew becomes dry while cooking. This should be a moist, thick curry.

TO SERVE Just before serving, remove cinnamon stick and cloves. Stir in cilantro. Ladle equal amounts of curry into each bowl.

WINE We enjoy this dish with the spiciness of a Zinfandel.

CORIANDER AND BLACK CARDAMOM
LAMB IN BUTTERMILK CURRY

 FROM A VISUAL point of view, this curry won't win any prizes. It is, however, the most satisfying stewed meat curry with a twist: we only use whole spices here.

We have based this dish loosely on a recipe given to Vikram's mother by her neighbour in Delhi in 1966. Vikram's mom never made it but she remembered enough bits and pieces of it that we were able to create this recipe. All she remembers about the neighbours is that they were from Rajasthan.

You can also use beef instead of lamb and it will be just as delicious. The longer the whole spices cook, the better the curry will taste. Serve this curry with rice pilaf or naan.

Serves 6 to 8

POUR BUTTERMILK into a large mixing bowl. Add lamb (or beef) and mix well. Cover the bowl with plastic wrap and refrigerate for at least 6 hours.

Lightly pound coriander seeds in a mortar or in a bowl with a heavy spoon. (You just want to crack the seeds in half.) Set aside.

Heat oil in a pot on medium heat for 1 minute. Add cumin seeds and cook until they sizzle for 30 to 45 seconds. Add garlic and sauté for 5 minutes, or until golden. Add coriander, chilies, cloves, black cardamom and salt. Stir well and cook for 3 to 4 minutes.

Add marinated meat with all the buttermilk plus 1 cup water. Stir continuously and bring to a boil. Reduce the heat to medium-low, cover and cook for about 1 hour. Remove the lid and stir in mashed potato. Cover the pot again and cook for another hour, or until meat is cooked and tender. (Continue cooking on low heat for as long as is necessary to cook the meat—just make sure it is covered in liquid, so add more water if needed. The longer you cook this curry, the better the spices will taste.)

TO SERVE You may want to take out the cloves before serving, or at least let your guests know to expect the cloves. Divide the curry equally among six or eight bowls.

WINE A Cabernet Franc from the Loire Valley is great with the black cardamom.

4 cups buttermilk, plus 1 cup water

3 lbs lamb leg or stewing beef, fat trimmed, in 2-inch cubes

2 Tbsp coriander seeds

½ cup canola oil

1½ Tbsp cumin seeds

3 Tbsp chopped garlic

ten to fifteen 2-inch pieces of dried red chilies

15 cloves

seeds from 10 black cardamom pods

1 Tbsp salt

10 oz potato (1 large), mashed

MARINATED LAMB POPSICLES
WITH FENUGREEK CREAM CURRY

 HIS IS OUR signature dish at Vij's—probably our most famous and most popular. The size of the lamb popsicles will depend on the rack of lamb you buy. If the popsicles are bigger, then four per serving is usually enough; if they are slightly smaller, then go with five per serving. Serve these popsicles over turmeric new potatoes (page 166).

Serves 6

LAMB Combine wine, mustard, salt and pepper in a large bowl. Add lamb and coat well with the marinade. Cover the bowl with plastic wrap and refrigerate for 2 to 4 hours.

CURRY SAUCE In a large bowl, combine cream, salt, paprika, cayenne, fenugreek leaves and lemon juice. Heat 3 to 4 Tbsp of the oil in a medium pot on medium heat and sauté garlic until golden. Stir in turmeric and cook for 1 minute. Stir in the cream mixture and cook on low to medium heat for about 5 minutes, or until it is gently boiling.

FINISH LAMB Preheat a stove-top cast iron grill or barbeque to high heat. Place lamb on the grill and cook for 2 to 3 minutes per side.

TO SERVE Serve popsicles piping hot off the grill. Depending on their size, place 4 to 5 lamb popsicles on each plate. Pour the cream curry over the meat or ladle it into a small bowl and use it as a dipping sauce for the popsicles.

WINE We love the Schloss Gobelsburg Grüner Veltliner, which we always keep on our wine list.

LAMB

¼ cup sweet white wine

¾ cup grainy yellow mustard

1 tsp salt

1 tsp ground black pepper

4 lbs French-cut racks of lamb, in chops

CURRY SAUCE

4 cups whipping cream

1 Tbsp salt

1 tsp paprika

½ tsp ground cayenne pepper

1 Tbsp dried green fenugreek leaves

¼ cup lemon juice

3 to 4 Tbsp canola oil

3 Tbsp finely chopped garlic

1 tsp turmeric

OVEN-BRAISED GOAT MEAT
IN FENNEL AND KALONJI CURRY

GOAT MEAT

1 lb leg of goat meat

2 lbs tomatoes, chopped
(about 4 large)

2 medium onions, chopped

1 Tbsp salt

½ Tbsp ground cayenne
pepper

½ tsp ground black pepper

1 Tbsp garam masala
(page 26)

4 cups water

**FENNEL AND
KALONJI CURRY**

2 Tbsp fennel seeds

1 Tbsp cumin seeds

1 tsp kalonji

1 tsp ajwain

½ cup canola oil

3 cups puréed tomatoes
(6 large)

1 Tbsp salt

½ tsp turmeric

½ tsp ground
cayenne pepper

4½ cups water

HIS IS A mild yet gamey curry for those who enjoy the richness of the meat but the mildness of the curry. It's hard to tell how much meat you will get from a leg of goat meat, but we are estimating that this recipe will make at least eight servings, if not more. You can always save what's left over and eat it the next day, when it will actually taste better since the shredded goat meat from the bones will soak up the flavours of the curry even more. You don't need to be precise about the size of onions or tomatoes in this recipe. We serve this curry with plain basmati rice or a rice pilaf.

Serves 8

GOAT MEAT Preheat the oven to 425°F. Trim off and discard the fat from the leg of goat meat. Place leg in a large roasting pan and mix in tomatoes, onions, salt, cayenne, black pepper, garam masala and water. Cover with a lid or seal tightly with aluminum foil, and cook for 2 hours. Remove the pan from the oven and allow meat to cool.

FENNEL AND KALONJI CURRY In a small frying pan, combine fennel, cumin, kalonji and ajwain. Cook on medium heat, stirring constantly, until fennel changes from green to having a yellowish tinge. This will take 2 to 3 minutes once the pan is warm. Turn off the heat and pour spices into a bowl to cool, for about 20 minutes. Grind cooled spices in a spice or coffee grinder.

While the spices are cooling, combine oil and tomatoes in a medium to large pot on medium-high heat. Add the ground spice mixture, salt, turmeric and cayenne, then stir and cook for 5 to 8 minutes, or until the oil separates from the masala. Add water and stir well. Bring to a boil, then reduce heat to low and simmer for 10 minutes. Turn off heat and set aside.

FINISH GOAT MEAT Wearing latex gloves, peel goat meat off the bone (make sure you get all the meat stuck on the bone). Discard the bone and stir meat back into the curry in which it cooked. Place the roasting pan on the stove and bring to a boil on medium-high heat. Remove the lid and boil for about 10 minutes, until there is enough liquid to keep goat meat, onions and tomatoes moist, but the mixture is not soupy.

FINISH FENNEL AND KALONJI CURRY Turn on the heat to medium and add goat meat, including the tomato and onion curry in which it was cooked. Mix well, and heat curry until it begins to boil.

TO SERVE Divide curry evenly among eight bowls. Serve immediately.

WINE Try a New World Cabernet Franc, particularly from either Washington State or Ontario.

SPICE-ENCRUSTED PORK

4 lbs whole
boneless pork rump
(about 3 lbs trimmed)
or 3 lbs pork loin
or shoulder

½ cup canola oil

1 Tbsp cumin seeds

4 Tbsp crushed garlic

1 cup puréed onions (1 large)

2 Tbsp crushed ginger

1 cup puréed
tomatoes (2 large)

1 tsp turmeric

1 tsp ground cayenne pepper

1½ Tbsp garam masala
(page 26)

1½ Tbsp salt

3 Tbsp raw sugar

OR THIS RECIPE, it doesn't matter if you use pork loin, pork shoulder or pork rump. The biggest difference is that it is easier to overcook the pork loin, whereas the pork shoulder or rump will stay juicy.

For this recipe, we have used pork rump roast. Depending on how much fat you trim off, the weight of the pork may decrease. We've developed this recipe for six servings with the fat trimmed off. So, if you use pork loin and it doesn't have very much fat on it, then use less than four pounds. Just let your butcher know that you need enough for six servings.

This is a dry pork curry with very little liquid. Therefore, unless you are serving it with another liquid curry or raita, it is best eaten with naan. A green salad with vinaigrette is also a nice complement.

Serves 6

TRIM OFF and discard the fat from the pork. Cut meat in 2-inch cubes. (Depending on where the fat is, some pieces will be larger than others.)

Heat oil in a medium-large pot on medium heat for 1 minute. Add cumin seeds and allow them to sizzle for 1 minute. Add garlic and sauté for 2 minutes, then stir in onions and sauté until brown, about 15 minutes. Add ginger and sauté for another 2 minutes. Stir in tomatoes, turmeric, cayenne, garam masala and salt, cover and cook for 5 minutes. Puréed tomatoes don't have much water in them, so covering the pan creates steam that prevents the tomatoes from sticking to the bottom of the pan and burning while cooking the spices. This is helpful, since we don't add any water here.

Stir in pork, cover and cook for 50 minutes, stirring every 15 minutes. If the pork or the masala is sticking to the bottom and might burn, stir in ¼ cup of water and slightly reduce the heat to medium-low.

Remove the lid and stir in raw sugar. Continue stirring and cooking for 3 to 5 minutes, or until sugar is completely dissolved.

TO SERVE Place equal portions of pork on each of six plates.

WINE We like to serve a German Riesling Kabinett to match the strong spices in this dish.

PORK TENDERLOIN
WITH SPINACH AND FIG STEW

CHICKEN STOCK

1 lb 6 oz chicken bones

13 cups water

1 large onion, chopped

3 carrots with
greens, chopped

2 tsp salt

½ tsp ground black pepper

PORK TENDERLOIN

½ cup canola oil

1 tsp salt

1 tsp ground black pepper

2 pork tenderloins, in 1-inch
slices (about 1 lb 13 oz)

canola oil for frying

 HIS IS A hearty, thick curry—it isn't soupy. You need a total of 8 cups of stock/water, so depending on how much chicken stock you make, you may need to add additional water. If you prefer a more soup-like curry, then add one more cup of water.

Tenderloin should only be grilled or seared, so we don't cook the pork in the stew. Instead, we pour the stew over the seared tenderloins in a large bowl. Two pork tenderloins give six generous or eight regular servings.

We have chosen spinach as the vegetable in this recipe, but you can use whichever vegetables you prefer as long as you add the potatoes. In this curry, the potatoes are meant to be very soft, so add the vegetables after the potatoes are cooked. Also, we don't brown the onions, so we get a sweeter onion flavour.

Serves 6 to 8

CHICKEN STOCK Combine chicken bones, water, onions, carrots and greens, salt and black pepper in a large pot with a lid. Bring to a boil on medium heat. Reduce the heat to low, cover and simmer for at least 2 hours. Check that there is enough water in the pot to keep the bones and vegetables covered at all times. Turn off the heat and allow the stock to cool.

Set a fine-mesh sieve over another pot or a stainless steel bowl. Using a ladle, strain chicken stock into the pot (or bowl) and discard solids. You should have about 6 cups of stock. Set aside. (Will keep in the refrigerator for up to 3 to 4 days, or frozen for up to 1 month, in a sealed container.)

PORK TENDERLOIN In a large mixing bowl, combine oil, salt and black pepper. Set the marinade aside.

You should have about thirty to thirty-two 1-inch slices of pork tenderloin. With a mallet, gently pound each slice of pork 4 to 5 times. Each piece should flatten a little. Mix pork in the marinade, making sure to coat the pieces well. Cover the bowl with plastic wrap and refrigerate for at least 3 hours.

STEW Heat oil in a medium or large pan on medium to high heat for 1 minute. Add cumin seeds and cook until they sizzle for 30 seconds. Add garlic and sauté for 2 to 3 minutes, or until light golden. Reduce the heat to medium, add onions and sauté until completely soft but not yet browned, about 5 minutes.

Add salt, garam masala, cayenne and turmeric. Stir well and cook for 5 minutes. Add figs and cook for another minute. Add potatoes and sauté for 3 to 4 minutes, stirring regularly. If the potatoes start to stick to the bottom of the pan, you may have to add a few tablespoons of water. Add stock. Bring to a boil, cover and cook for 8 to 10 minutes, or until potatoes are cooked through.

FINISH PORK TENDERLOIN Heat a large nonstick frying pan on medium heat for 1 minute. Add enough oil to lightly cover the bottom. Add as many marinated pork slices as you can to the frying pan. You may want to sear the pork in serving portions, that is, 4 or 8 slices at a time. Cook on one side for about 1½ minutes, until the outside is slightly crispy. Turn slices over and cook for another 1½ minutes.

FINISH STEW Just before serving, stir in the spinach and cook for 1 minute, until the leaves have wilted into the stew.

TO SERVE Arrange 4 slices of pork on each plate or shallow bowl for 8 servings, or 5 slices of pork for 6 servings. Pour an equal amount of spinach and potato stew over each serving.

WINE A Loire Valley Chenin Blanc is best with this milder curry.

STEW

½ cup canola oil

1 Tbsp cumin seeds

3 Tbsp thinly sliced garlic

2 medium onions, thinly sliced

1 Tbsp salt

1 Tbsp + 1 tsp garam masala (page 26)

½ tsp ground cayenne pepper

1 tsp turmeric

7 dried figs, chopped

1 large + 1 medium russet potato, peeled and cut in ½-inch dice

6 cups chicken stock

10 oz spinach (1 bunch), washed, de-stemmed and coarsely chopped

Poultry

VIJ FAMILY'S CHICKEN CURRY

½ cup canola oil

2 cups finely chopped
onions (2 large)

3-inch stick of cinnamon

3 Tbsp finely chopped garlic

2 Tbsp chopped ginger

2 cups chopped tomatoes
(2 large)

1 Tbsp salt

½ tsp ground black pepper

1 tsp turmeric

1 Tbsp ground cumin

1 Tbsp ground coriander

1 Tbsp garam masala
(page 26)

½ tsp ground
cayenne pepper

3 lbs chicken thighs, bone in

1 cup sour cream, stirred

2 cups water

½ cup chopped cilantro
(including stems)

 HIS WAS THE original chicken curry Vikram's mom used to make in his apartment when he first opened Vij's in 1994 and didn't have the appropriate licences to cook in the newly acquired café. This curry is based on a family recipe, except that she added sour cream to make it richer. If you want a lighter curry, you can take the sour cream out of this recipe altogether.

When making a stewed chicken curry, we always cook with dark meat (breast meat dries too quickly) and with the bone in. The advantage of cooking the curry with boned chicken is that it makes for a heartier stock and allows the chicken to simmer in its own juices. Serve with naan or rice.

Serves 6

IN A LARGE PAN, heat oil on medium heat for 1 minute. Add onions and cinnamon, and sauté for 5 to 8 minutes, until onions are golden. Add garlic and sauté for another 4 minutes. Add ginger, tomatoes, salt, black pepper, turmeric, cumin, coriander, garam masala and cayenne. Cook this masala for 5 minutes, or until the oil separates from the masala.

Remove and discard skin from the chicken thighs. Wash thighs and add to the masala. Stir well. Cook chicken thighs for 10 minutes, until the chicken looks cooked on the outside. Add sour cream and water and stir well. Increase the heat to medium-high. When curry starts to boil, reduce the heat to medium, cover and cook for 15 minutes, stirring 2 or 3 times, until chicken is completely cooked. Poke the thighs with a knife. If the meat is still pink, cook for 5 more minutes. Remove and discard the cinnamon stick. Cool curry for at least half an hour.

Transfer cooled chicken to a mixing bowl. Wearing latex gloves, peel chicken meat off the bones. Discard bones and stir chicken back into the curry. Just before serving, heat curry on medium heat until it starts to boil lightly. Stir in cilantro.

TO SERVE Divide curry evenly among six bowls.

WINE A Spanish Tempranillo with good fruit and balanced tannins is a great complement to this curry.

GRILLED CHICKEN

BE SURE TO use boneless chicken thighs for this recipe, as breast meat doesn't soak in the flavours of the yogurt and tamarind. If your tamarind paste has the texture of a fruit smoothie rather than a thick jam, use 2 Tbsp instead of 1 Tbsp. Since this particular chicken dish almost feels like a hearty finger food, we always serve it with another curry or a pilaf. We suggest the Semolina Noodles with Vegetables and Lentils (page 151) or the Coconut Curried Vegetables (page 142) with basmati rice (page 167). At a minimum, serve this chicken on lots of greens with an oil and vinegar dressing.

Serves 6

¾ cup plain yogurt, stirred

1 Tbsp tamarind paste (page 32)

3 Tbsp finely chopped garlic

¼ cup canola oil

1½ Tbsp salt

1¼ tsp ground cayenne pepper

1 Tbsp garam masala (page 26)

2¼ lbs boneless chicken thighs (about 6 oz per serving)

1 lemon, in 6 wedges (optional)

IN A LARGE mixing bowl, combine yogurt, tamarind paste, garlic, oil, salt, cayenne and garam masala. Add chicken thighs and mix well. Make sure chicken is well covered in the marinade. Cover the bowl with plastic wrap and refrigerate for at least 4 hours and up to 8 hours. The longer the chicken marinates, the stronger the flavours will be.

Preheat a grill, barbeque or stovetop cast-iron grill to high heat. Remember to turn on your exhaust fan if you are grilling on your stovetop, since the cooking process will emit some smoke. Grill marinated chicken thighs on one side for about 2 minutes and then turn over. Grill the other side for 2 minutes and turn over again. Grill each side again for 2 minutes, for a total of 4 minutes per side. Poke the thighs with a knife to be sure they are cooked through. If the meat is still pink, grill each side for 1 minute more.

TO SERVE Divide rice, noodles or salad greens among six plates. Top with grilled chicken. While piping hot, squeeze a little fresh lemon, according to taste, on the chicken. If serving with the coconut curried vegetables, you can put the vegetables on the same plate as the chicken or in small side bowls.

WINE A Tavel Rosé from France goes really well with the grilled, tangy flavours of this dish.

CILANTRO-MINT CHICKEN CURRY

CILANTRO-MINT CHUTNEY

2 cups chopped cilantro

⅔ cup chopped mint leaves

2 jalapeño peppers,
finely chopped

1½ cups chopped red onion
(about 1 large)

1 Tbsp chopped ginger

⅓ tsp asafoetida

1 cup (approximately) water

ECAUSE VERY FEW spices are used in this recipe and because its flavour rests on the green chutney, the amount of the cilantro, mint, jalapeño pepper and red onion matters. Use the leaves and stems of the cilantro, but discard the stems of the mint and use only the mint leaves.

As for the chicken, we prefer to use chicken thighs with the bone in, let the bones cook in the curry for heartiness, and then peel the cooled chicken and discard the bones. For convenience and to save time, you can also buy boneless chicken thighs.

Serve with plain basmati rice or plain naan. This is a delicate curry in comparison to the others, but the green chutney gives it a wonderful zing. If you serve it with a rice pilaf that contains other spices, you will lose the focus on the flavour of the chicken.

Serves 6

CILANTRO-MINT CHUTNEY Mix cilantro leaves and stems, mint leaves, jalapeño peppers, onions, ginger and asafoetida in a large bowl. Pour one-third of this mixture into a blender with ⅓ cup of the water. Purée until smooth. Transfer to a bowl. Repeat two more times with the remaining cilantro-mint mixture and water. You should have a green chutney. Set aside while you prepare the curry.

CURRY Heat oil in a heavy, shallow pot (make sure it has a tight-fitting lid) on medium heat for 1 minute. Add cumin and coriander seeds and allow them to sizzle for about 30 seconds (the cumin will actually sizzle, the coriander will just cook). Add garlic and sauté for about 3 minutes, or until golden brown. Stir in salt. Turn off the heat and after 2 to 3 minutes, stir in yogurt (or buttermilk). Add chicken thighs and stir well. Turn the heat to medium, then cover and cook for about 25 minutes, stirring regularly. Remove curry from the heat and cool for about 20 minutes.

Transfer cooled chicken to a mixing bowl. Wearing latex gloves, peel chicken meat off the bones. The size of the chicken pieces doesn't matter but do not shred them. Discard the bones and stir chicken back into the curry. Stir in the cilantro-mint chutney. About 15 minutes before serving, bring curry to a boil on medium heat. Turn down the heat to simmer and cook, uncovered, for about 10 minutes, or until chicken is well mixed with chutney.

TO SERVE Place ½ cup of cooked rice in each of six large bowls. Ladle chicken curry over the rice. Or, serve chicken in smaller bowls with naan on a side plate.

WINE A New World Semillon is very versatile and will pair well with the yogurt and the mint.

CURRY

½ cup canola oil

1½ Tbsp cumin seeds

1 Tbsp coriander seeds

3 Tbsp crushed garlic

1 Tbsp salt

1 cup plain yogurt, stirred, or ¾ cup whole-fat buttermilk

3 lbs chicken thighs, bone in

3 cups cooked basmati rice

TAMARIND-MARINATED
CHICKEN BREAST
IN COCONUT-CHICKPEA FLOUR CURRY

CHICKEN MARINADE

2¼ lbs boneless chicken breasts (about 6 oz per serving), lightly poked all over with a knife

⅔ cup tamarind paste (page 32)

2 Tbsp chopped garlic

¾ cup canola oil

3 Tbsp sugar

1 tsp ground cayenne pepper

1 Tbsp Mexican chili powder

1 Tbsp paprika (optional)

1½ Tbsp salt

CURRY

½ cup canola oil

1½ lbs onions (2 large), thinly sliced

7 large garlic cloves (1 oz), thinly sliced lengthwise

8 oz tomatoes, finely chopped (2 medium)

1 large jalapeño pepper, chopped

½ Tbsp ground cumin

2 Tbsp ground coriander

1 tsp crushed cayenne pepper

1 tsp turmeric

1½-inch whole cinnamon stick

1½ Tbsp salt

5 Tbsp chickpea flour

6 cups water

1 cup coconut milk, stirred

BECAUSE THE CHICKEN is grilled, we use lots of oil in the marinade. We also use paprika just to give the brown colour of the tamarind a reddish tone. The use of paprika is optional. At Vij's, we serve this chicken topped with Bitter Melon with Paneer and Raw Sugar (page 138).

Serves 6

CHICKEN MARINADE Cut each chicken breast in half horizontally and trim off the fat.

Combine tamarind paste, garlic, oil, sugar, cayenne, chili powder, paprika and salt in a large bowl. Add chicken breasts and mix well. Make sure chicken is well covered in the marinade. Cover the bowl with plastic wrap and refrigerate for 3 hours.

CURRY Heat oil in a pot on medium heat for 1 minute. Add onions and sauté until brown, about 10 minutes. Add garlic and sauté for another 3 to 4 minutes, until golden brown. Some of the onions will seem slightly burned at the edges, and this will actually add flavour. Stir in tomatoes, jalapeño pepper, cumin, coriander, cayenne, turmeric, cinnamon stick and salt and cook for 5 to 8 minutes, or until oil glistens through the tomatoes. Reduce the heat to low.

In a separate mixing bowl, combine chickpea flour and 1 cup of the water and mix thoroughly with a whisk. Make sure there are no lumps. Add this chickpea mixture and the remaining water to the curry. Stir well and increase the heat to medium. Once curry starts to boil, reduce the heat to low. Add coconut milk. While stirring regularly, simmer curry for 20 to 25 minutes. The curry will thicken as it boils because of the chickpea flour. Cook until it has the consistency of a cream sauce.

FINISH CHICKEN Preheat a stovetop flat-iron grill or barbeque to high heat. (If using the stovetop grill, turn on your kitchen exhaust fan.) Grill each chicken breast half on one side for 4 to 5 minutes. Turn chicken over and grill for another 4 to 5 minutes. Gently poke the breasts with a knife to be sure they are cooked through. If the meat is still pink, grill each side for 1 minute more.

TO SERVE Place equal portions of grilled chicken breast on each plate. Pour about ½ cup of piping hot curry over each serving.

WINE A northern Italian red such as a Dolcetto d'Alba is lovely with the coconut–chickpea flour curry and the sweet and tart flavours of the tamarind.

PANFRIED TOMATO AND CORIANDER
QUAIL CAKES

12 quails

13 cups cold water

2 large potatoes
(any kind), peeled

1 Tbsp crushed
cayenne pepper

1 Tbsp salt

½ cup chopped cilantro

⅓ cup + 1 Tbsp canned
ground tomatoes

1 egg, beaten

2 to 4 Tbsp canola oil

W E USED TO serve whole quails in a curry but found that it was quite messy for our customers to get the meat off the bones, even if we offered a bowl of hot water and lemon afterwards. Shredded quail meat in a curry often leaves the meat overcooked, so we came up with these cakes as an easy but delicious way to eat quail. We use the water in which we boil the quails as a stock for our chicken curry.

You can serve these cakes with chutneys and naan as an appetizer or as part of a main course, either with the Cauliflower and Potato Purée (page 165) or with the Semolina Noodles with Vegetables and Lentils (page 151). Be sure to serve naan or rice if you are making a vegetable curry.

Serves 6

PLACE QUAILS and 8 cups of the water in a large pot. Bring to a boil on high heat and boil for 5 minutes. Make sure you do not overboil the quails, as the meat will become tough and overcooked. Drain water and reserve as stock. Allow quails to cool in the pot.

Combine potatoes and remaining 5 cups of the water in a separate pot. Bring to a boil on medium-high heat and boil for 45 minutes, or until potatoes are soft enough to mash. Drain water and allow potatoes to cool.

Wearing latex gloves, remove and discard the skin from the quail. Peel quail meat off the bones (be sure to get into the nooks and crannies). Shred, then finely chop the meat. Discard the bones. Mash the potatoes.

In a large mixing bowl, combine chopped quail meat, mashed potatoes, cayenne, salt, cilantro, tomatoes and egg. Form the mixture in patties 2 inches in diameter and ½ inch thick.

Heat a nonstick frying pan on medium-high heat. Add 1 tsp of oil, heat, then panfry 2 to 4 cakes on one side for 2 to 3 minutes, or until cakes sizzle and become lightly crispy. Add more oil if the cakes begin to stick to the pan as you fry them. Turn cakes over and cook for another 2 to 3 minutes. Remember that all ingredients have already been cooked, so cook them just enough that they are hot on the inside and crispy on the outside. Repeat with the remaining cakes, adding 1 tsp of oil for every 2 to 4 cakes.

TO SERVE Place 2 quail cakes on each plate, with chutney and naan arranged on the same plate. If you are serving these cakes with a vegetable curry, serve the vegetable curry in small side bowls. If serving with semolina noodles, place 2 quail cakes on top of equal portions of noodles on each plate.

WINE We serve a New World Pinot Noir with these quail cakes. Try a British Columbia variety, if it's available.

DUCK BREAST IN LIME LEAF CURRY

INCE DUCK IS a gamey, heavier meat, we came up with this crisp, refreshing curry. We want this curry to have a mellow lemon flavour rather than the tartness of lemon juice, so we use lime leaves and lemon grass instead of fresh lemons. As lime leaves are used in many Thai and Southeast Asian dishes, you can buy these ingredients from most Asian grocers but not necessarily from an Indian grocer. The intensity of the lemon flavour will depend on the quality of the lemon grass and lime leaves you use.

Once you've seared the duck breast pieces, serve this dish immediately. Serve this curry with naan or with the Ginger, Jalapeño and Coconut Brown Rice Pilaf (page 170).

Serves 6

....

LIME LEAF CURRY Using a sharp knife, cut off the top 8 inches of the lemon grass stalks. Discard the thinner, drier bottom parts of the stalks. Lightly pound lemon grass with a mallet, and then chop it in pieces ¼ to ½ inch long.

Combine lemon grass and 4 cups of the water in a pot and bring to a boil on high heat. Reduce the heat to low, cover and simmer for half an hour. Turn off the heat and allow water and lemon grass to remain in the pot until lukewarm.

Place a fine-mesh sieve over another pot or a bowl. Strain lemon grass water into the pot (or bowl) and discard solids. You should have about 2½ cups of lemon grass water. Set aside.

Heat oil in a pot on medium heat for 1 minute. Stir in onions and sauté for 10 minutes, or until brown. Add garlic and sauté for another 3 minutes. Add tomatoes, salt, turmeric, garam masala and paprika and cook for 5 minutes, or until oil glistens on top. Add the remaining 2½ cups of water, the lemon grass water, coconut milk and lime leaves. Stir well and bring to a boil. Reduce the heat to low and boil gently for 10 to 15 minutes.

LIME LEAF CURRY

4½ oz lemon grass
(3 long stalks)

6½ cups water

½ cup canola oil

2 cups puréed onions
(2 large)

3 Tbsp finely chopped garlic

⅔ cup canned
crushed tomatoes

1 Tbsp + 1 tsp salt

1 tsp turmeric

1½ Tbsp garam masala
(page 26)

1 tsp paprika

2 cups coconut milk, stirred

15 lime leaves

6 duck breasts (with skin)

½ tsp salt

1 to 1½ Tbsp orange zest

¼ cup canola oil

DUCK While the curry is boiling, wash each duck breast under cold water for a few seconds.

Heat a heavy frying pan on high for 3 minutes. Keeping your face at a distance, place duck breast(s), skin side down, in the frying pan. The duck will immediately make a loud sizzling noise. Still keeping your face at a distance, sprinkle a pinch of salt and a large pinch of orange zest on each breast. Within 1 to 2 minutes, you should see fat coming out of the duck (just as you do with bacon). Sear each duck breast on one side for 3 to 4 minutes. Turn duck breast over and sear for another 3 to 4 minutes. Cool duck breast(s) enough that you can touch them.

Slice each duck breast in ¾-inch pieces. The meat will be red in the centre, and you should have 5 to 6 pieces per breast. If you are not serving the duck immediately, set aside, cover and refrigerate it until you are ready.

Line a plate with paper towel. Drain and wipe the frying pan in which you seared the duck breasts or use a new frying pan. Add 1 tsp of the oil and heat on medium-high heat. Add 5 to 6 pieces of duck breast and sear on one side for 1 minute. Turn duck pieces over and cook for 1 minute more, or until meat is light pink in the centre. Repeat with the remaining pieces, adding more oil if necessary so the duck does not stick to the pan. As the seared duck pieces are cooked, place them on the paper towel–lined plate.

TO SERVE If you are serving this with plain rice or the coconut brown rice pilaf, place equal portions of rice in six large, shallow bowls first. Arrange 5 to 6 pieces of duck breast on top of the rice or in each bowl. Pour hot curry over the duck breast. We serve the duck breast with the crispy skin and leave it to individual preferences whether or not the skin is eaten.

WINE We recommend an Old World Pinot Noir, to go with the gamey flavour of the duck.

GRILLED CHICKEN BREAST

MARINATED IN LEMON-GHEE DRESSING WITH ROASTED GARLIC
AND CASHEWS AND SPICY TOMATO CURRY

CHICKEN

2¼ lbs chicken breasts (6 oz per serving), lightly poked all over with a knife

3 oz fresh lemon juice (2 juicy lemons)

½ Tbsp salt

½ Tbsp ground cayenne pepper

2 tsp paprika

1 Tbsp ground coriander

1 Tbsp ground cumin

½ cup ghee (page 30), melted

TOMATO CURRY

⅓ cup canola oil

15 to 20 curry leaves

½ tsp asafoetida

1 Tbsp canned ground tomatoes

¼ tsp turmeric

2 tsp salt

½ tsp ground cayenne

½ tsp ground fenugreek

3½ cups tomato broth (page 31)

2 to 3 cups water

THE AMOUNT OF garlic used in this recipe may seem shocking, but the garlic shrinks down when baked in the oven. It then gives a lovely flavour when mixed with ghee. You will need to marinate the chicken for about 3 hours. You will also have to make the garlic and cashews and the lemon-ghee dressing before you grill the chicken.

We serve this chicken dish with a spicy tomato curry, which is actually very light on the spices though the cayenne pepper gives it heat. The cayenne complements the tangy tomato, which in turn tastes great with the tart lemon-ghee dressing. You can serve the tomato curry on its own with a bowl of basmati rice, as a light meal.

Be sure to make the tomato curry first and have it piping hot and ready to serve once the chicken is grilled. Serve with rice.

Serves 6

CHICKEN Cut chicken breasts in half horizontally, then trim off and discard the fat. Combine lemon juice, salt, cayenne, paprika, coriander, cumin and ghee in a large bowl. Add chicken breasts and mix well. Make sure chicken is well covered in the marinade. Cover the bowl with plastic wrap and refrigerate for 3 hours.

TOMATO CURRY Heat oil in a medium-large frying pan on medium heat for 1 minute. Add curry leaves and cook for 30 seconds. Keep your head away from the curry leaves, as they may splatter. They will shrivel up a bit. Add asafoetida and cook for 30 seconds, then turn off the heat. (The oil is very hot at this point and could burn the spices.) After 1 minute, add tomatoes and stir. Add turmeric, salt, cayenne and fenugreek. Stir and turn the heat to medium. Cook the masala for 4 to 5 minutes, or until oil glistens on top.

Stir in tomato broth and 2 cups of the water. Bring to a boil, reduce the heat to low, cover and cook for 15 minutes, stirring every 5 minutes. The curry should have the consistency of tomato soup. If it is too thick, add ½ to 1 cup more water. Otherwise, turn off the heat and set aside until you are ready to serve the chicken.

GARLIC AND CASHEWS Preheat the oven or toaster oven to 375°F. In a small bowl, thoroughly combine garlic, salt, cayenne and black pepper. Spread the coated garlic on a small baking tray and bake for 3 to 4 minutes. Lightly stir garlic to cook it evenly. Return to the oven for another 3 or 4 minutes, or until garlic is golden and slightly darker around the edges. Watch carefully to be sure garlic does not burn. Remove from the oven and set aside.

Spread cashews in a single layer on a small baking tray and bake for 4 to 5 minutes. Lightly stir cashews to cook them evenly. Return to the oven for another 4 or 5 minutes, or until cashews darken around the edges. Watch carefully to be sure cashews are not burning. Remove from the oven. Chop cashews in quarters.

Mix the roasted garlic and cashews in a small bowl and set aside.

LEMON-GHEE DRESSING Heat ghee in a small heavy pot on medium heat. Add lemon juice and immediately reduce heat to low.

FINISH CHICKEN Preheat a barbeque or a stovetop flat-iron grill to high heat. (If using the stovetop grill, turn on your kitchen exhaust fan.) Grill each chicken breast on one side for 4 to 5 minutes. Turn chicken over and grill for another 4 to 5 minutes, or until chicken is cooked through. Gently poke the breasts with a knife to be sure they are cooked through. If the meat is still pink, grill each side for 1 minute more. While still on the grill, glaze both sides of the chicken with the lemon-ghee dressing.

TO SERVE Divide grilled chicken breasts evenly among six plates. Top with equal portions of the garlic-cashew mixture. Pour ½ cup of piping hot tomato curry around the chicken.

WINE A smooth white Burgundy nicely balances the garlic and the lemon-ghee dressing.

GARLIC AND CASHEWS

½ cup garlic cloves, thinly sliced in round pieces

1 tsp salt

½ tsp ground cayenne pepper

⅓ tsp ground black pepper

3 oz whole raw cashews

....

LEMON-GHEE DRESSING

¼ cup ghee (page 30)

2 oz fresh lemon juice (1 to 1½ juicy lemons)

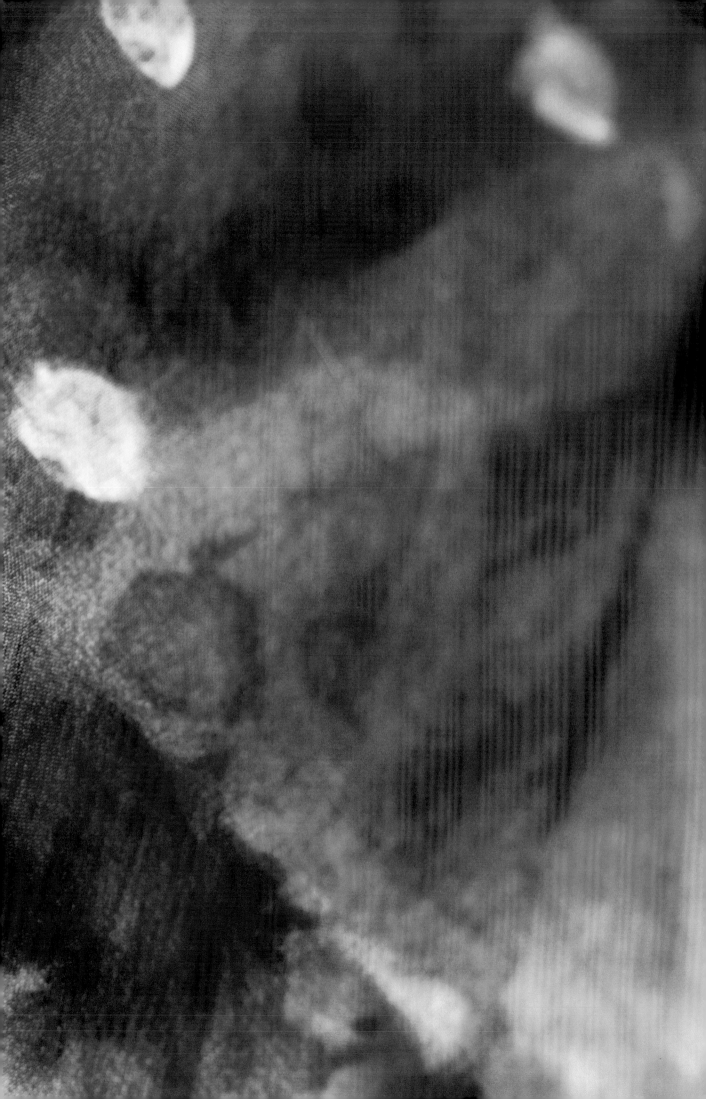

MAINS

Fish & Seafood

WHEN WE OPENED Vij's in 1994, we focussed on seafood that not only tasted good with Indian spices but also kept its texture during the cooking process. We first served a yogurt-marinated cod on cauliflower rice pilaf. Affordable and relatively easy to sear *à la minute*, the cod became the most popular item on our menu during the spring of 1995. From cod, we moved to salmon, which we grilled on skewers. More and more of our customers, especially women, were ordering seafood instead of red meat, so we always made sure to have seafood dishes on our menu. After salmon, we started using tiger prawns and orange roughy.

One day, our manager told us that a prominent food critic in Vancouver had come in for dinner and commented that we were serving an endangered fish on our menu. That assertion hit us like a rock, as the issue really had never occurred to us.

We had very different responses. Vikram couldn't believe that an endangered fish would be sold in the market and set out to prove that orange roughy wasn't endangered. First, he contacted the distributor, who informed him that the fish was in good supply and that our orange roughy was from New Zealand. Vikram then contacted the government of New Zealand's Ministry of fisheries, who sent an email assuring us that orange roughy fisheries were being monitored and quotas were in place, so it was fine to serve it.

In contrast, Meeru contacted the Audubon Society and the Monterey Bay Aquarium in California, both of which confirmed *all* orange roughy was considered endangered.

At issue were the age and reproductive cycle of the fish: orange roughy live very deep in the ocean and live as long as 90 to 150 years. They don't start to reproduce until the age of 30 or so, and the number of offspring per fish is very low compared to other species. Orange roughy had been grossly overfished in Australia, Namibia and New Zealand. Many environmentalists and scientists believe that the success of new government quotas and procedures can't be assessed until the current population of orange roughy reaches its reproductive years. Also at issue was the method used to catch the deepwater fish: bottom trawling damages the ocean areas where the fish aggregate and it also collects other fish and sea animals that are then discarded overboard and left to die. After consulting our staff, we replaced the orange roughy with locally available Pacific halibut.

We also inadvertently discovered that imported tiger prawns were on these two organizations' list of of seafoods to be avoided, but not because they were endangered. Shrimp trawling had the highest by-catch of all the fisheries and for every pound of shrimp or prawns caught, up to 15 pounds of other sea animals were caught and then discarded.

Tiger prawns were even more popular with our customers than fish, and we kept them on the menu until we could reach a mutual decision with input from our staff. After researching and discussing the pros and cons from the business point of view, we replaced tiger prawns with B.C. spot prawns or California farmed prawns. This change meant that we had to raise our prices.

Despite the price increase, Vikram received an overwhelmingly positive response from our customers, many of whom were unaware of such issues. This gave us the confidence to decide that we would conscientiously determine what to offer our customers rather than just cater to popular demand.

Since then, we have joined the Vancouver Aquarium's Ocean Wise program (as have many Vancouver restaurants), which provides us with information on sustainable seafood choices. It didn't happen right away, but we did realize that, as restaurateurs, we play an important role in educating and sharing our views with our customers through our menu.

There are many resources available to consumers who want to make sustainable seafood choices. On the Internet, the Monterey Bay Aquarium, www.mbayaq.org, has an excellent Seafood Watch program, which lists all seafood in "best," "good" and "avoid" categories and the reasons why. The Audubon Society web site, http://seafood.audubon.org, has a seafood wallet card that you can download and print to carry with you while shopping or dining out.

SEARED STRIPED BASS

WITH SOUR CREAM CURRY

STRIPED BASS IS an enclosed farmed fish, also known as inland farmed fish, which means it is farmed away from coastal waters and doesn't pose a threat to other ocean fish. We decided to try striped bass as a substitute for Chilean sea bass (Patagonian toothfish), which is high on the endangered fish list. Although it obviously differs slightly from the Chilean sea bass, we find it easy to cook with and it goes very well with a variety of Indian spices.

The big difference between the two fish is that it is time consuming to cut the skin off the striped bass and so we cook with the skin on. If you don't like to eat the skin, it is easy to remove after cooking. However, most of our customers who profess not to eat fish skin have loved the crispiness and the spicing on this fish. Having been farmed inland, the striped bass will have no pollutants from the ocean in its skin. You can also save time by marinating the fish ahead of time. Cover the coated fillets with plastic wrap and refrigerate for up to 6 hours. Serve this curry with rice or naan.

Serves 6

SOUR CREAM CURRY Heat ½ cup of the oil in a pot on medium heat for 1 minute. Add asafoetida, stirring well, and allow to sizzle for 30 seconds. Stir in tomatoes and add salt, turmeric, cayenne and fenugreek. Reduce the heat to low, cover the pot and cook for 5 minutes. Remove the lid and stir well.

Add water, stir and increase the heat to medium. Bring to a boil and cook for 10 minutes, stirring regularly so the water blends in completely with the spices. Stir in sour cream and bring to a boil. Reduce the heat to low and cook for another 5 minutes. Remove from the heat.

In a separate small frying pan, heat the remaining ¼ cup oil on medium heat. Sauté garlic for about 5 minutes, or until brown but not burned. (You want to cook the garlic as much as possible without burning it.) Stir cooked garlic into the sour cream curry and set aside.

SOUR CREAM CURRY

¾ cup canola oil

1 tsp asafoetida

3 cups puréed tomatoes (6 large)

1 Tbsp salt

1 tsp turmeric

1 tsp ground cayenne pepper

2 tsp ground fenugreek seeds

7 cups water

1¼ cups sour cream, stirred

3 Tbsp crushed garlic

STRIPED BASS

6 fillets striped bass,
each 6 oz

½ Tbsp salt

1 Tbsp cumin seeds

1½ Tbsp ground cumin

2 Tbsp ground coriander

1 tsp turmeric

1 tsp ground
cayenne pepper

2 tsp paprika

1 Tbsp mango powder

½ cup canola oil for searing

STRIPED BASS Trim the white sides off each fish fillet, if this hasn't already been done. Using a large knife, scrape the fish scales off the skin, scraping away from the body. Feel with your hands to be sure no small scales remain on the skin. This shouldn't take more than 1 or 2 minutes per fillet, as the scales come off easily.

In a large bowl, mix salt, cumin seeds, ground cumin, coriander, turmeric, cayenne, paprika and mango powder. Spread this mixture on a baking tray. Dip each fillet in the mixed spices, making sure both sides of each piece are completely coated. Arrange coated fillets on the baking tray.

Just before serving, heat 1½ Tbsp of oil in a nonstick frying pan on medium heat. Place a fillet, skin side down, in the frying pan and cook for about 2 minutes. The skin should be slightly crispy. Gently turn the fillet over and cook for another 2 minutes. This fish doesn't take long to cook through. Once cooked, it will flake easily when pierced with a fork. Repeat with the remaining fillets, adding just enough oil so that the fish skin sizzles and is slightly crispy.

TO SERVE Arrange 1 striped bass fillet, skin side up, in each of six large bowls. Pour one-sixth of the sour cream curry over each serving.

WINE The richness of this dish needs a full-bodied white Bordeaux.

PRAWNS

IN COCONUT AND SAFFRON CURRY

I**T IS DIFFICULT** to pinpoint the measurement for saffron in any recipe, as the quality varies among brands. We use the deep red threads of Spanish saffron. If you buy saffron with lots of yellow-orange threads, you will need to use more than is listed in this recipe, as this is not a pure form of saffron. Having written that, good saffron is also very expensive and you can't always buy it at your local grocery store.

We strongly recommend that you use U.S.-farmed or wild-caught prawns rather than Asian tiger prawns. Due to the trawling techniques used, Asian tiger prawns are not considered an environmentally sustainable species for consumption. In British Columbia, we also cook with local spot prawns. Serve this dish with plain basmati rice or a rice pilaf or, as at Vij's, over Grilled Coconut Kale (page 162).

Serves 6

1 tsp saffron

½ cup lukewarm water

30 large prawns

1 Tbsp + 1 tsp salt

½ cup canola oil

1½ Tbsp cumin seeds

3 cups puréed tomatoes (6 large)

2 Tbsp ground black mustard seeds

1 tsp ground fenugreek seeds

½ Tbsp crushed cayenne pepper

1 tsp turmeric

4 cups water

2 cups coconut milk, stirred

IN A CUP or a bowl, soak saffron in lukewarm water for 20 minutes. Set aside.

Shell and devein prawns. In a large bowl, combine prawns and 1 tsp of the salt. Mix well with your hands. Cover the bowl with plastic wrap and refrigerate for up to 6 hours.

Heat oil in a shallow medium pot on high heat for 1 minute. Stir in cumin seeds and allow them to sizzle for about 30 seconds. Turn down the heat to medium, then add tomatoes, mustard seeds, fenugreek seeds, cayenne, turmeric and the 1 Tbsp of salt. Stir well and cook for 5 minutes, or until oil glistens on the tomatoes.

Add the 4 cups of water. Increase the heat to high and bring to a boil. Reduce the heat to medium-low and cook curry for another 10 minutes, stirring regularly. Add coconut milk and saffron (including its water). Stir well and cook for another 10 minutes.

Just before serving, bring the curry to a boil on medium heat. As soon as it starts boiling, add prawns but do not stir them immediately, as they may break or tear. After 1 minute, stir them gently. Cook for about 4 minutes, or until prawns are pinkish-orange. Be careful not to overcook the prawns.

TO SERVE Ladle prawn curry into six individual bowls and serve immediately.

WINE We serve a Verdejo from Spain to match the saffron.

SEARED PACIFIC HALIBUT

WITH BLACK CHICKPEA AND YAM CURRY

BLACK CHICKPEAS

2 cups dried black chickpeas

6 cups water for soaking

½ Tbsp salt

9 cups water for boiling

YAM STOCK

12 oz yam (1 large), peeled and cut in 1-inch cubes

11 cups water

14 oz tomatoes (2 large), chopped in 12 to 16 pieces

9 oz onion (1 large), chopped in 6 to 8 pieces

W E SEAR THE entire halibut fillet and serve it in a large bowl with the chickpea curry. It's quite filling (and nutritious!) as is, so this recipe is a complete meal with no need for any side dishes. Just one or two pieces of naan or even a baguette to soak up the soup will be enough. Since the shapes and sizes of yams vary so much, we've given its weight for the recipe. Do not use garnet yams, as they are too sweet and sometimes stringy and therefore don't blend into the curry as well.

You will need a food processor and lots of large mixing bowls and pans for this dish. Don't worry if this recipe seems to make a lot of curry: that's how we serve this dish, with lots of curry.

Serves 6

BLACK CHICKPEAS Wash the chickpeas and drain. In a large bowl or pan, combine chickpeas and the 6 cups of water and soak for at least 6 hours or overnight. Drain chickpeas and discard the soaking water.

In a large pot, combine chickpeas, salt and the 9 cups of water. Bring them to a boil on high heat. Reduce the heat to low, cover and simmer for 1 hour. The outer skin of black chickpeas is thicker than the skin of regular yellow chickpeas, so taste one or mash one between your fingers to be sure they are fully cooked. Remove from the heat and set aside. Do not drain the chickpeas.

YAM STOCK Place yam and water in a large pot with a tight-fitting lid. Add tomatoes and onions and bring to a boil on high heat. Reduce the heat to low, cover and simmer for 2 hours. Allow stock to cool completely.

Using a big ladle, transfer batches of yam, tomato and onion pieces to the bowl of a food processor. Purée all the pieces, then return them to the soup. Stir the mixture well. You should have a puréed soup with a velvety texture. Set aside.

CURRY Heat ghee in a large pot on medium to high heat for 1 minute. Sprinkle in mustard seeds and stir. Cook for 1 to 2 minutes, until you hear 1 or 2 popping sounds. (The popping sound means that a seed has burned, and you don't want more than a few burned seeds.) Add green onions and stir well to prevent mustard seeds from burning at the bottom of the pan. Sauté for 8 to 10 minutes, until green onions are dark brown and shrivelled. Add jalapeño peppers and ginger and sauté for another 5 minutes. Stir in wine and cook for 3 to 4 minutes. Add cumin and salt and cook for another 3 to 4 minutes.

Stir this masala into the chickpeas. Be sure to get all the masala by pouring some of the cooking water from the chickpeas into the masala pan, swirling it around and then emptying it back into the chickpeas. Stir well. Combine yam stock with curried chickpeas and stir well.

Just before you sear the fish, bring curry to a boil on medium heat. Once it is boiling, reduce the heat to low and allow it to simmer.

HALIBUT Combine salt and cayenne in a bowl. Using your hands, rub a little of this mixture onto both sides of each fillet. (You can use latex gloves if you wish to avoid the smell of the fish and spices on your hands.) Arrange the coated fillets on a baking tray or a plate.

In a small nonstick frying pan, heat 1 Tbsp of oil on medium to high heat for about 1 minute. Sear a fillet on one side for 2 to 3 minutes. The fish should be slightly crispy on the cooked side. Gently turn the fillet over and sear for another 2 to 3 minutes, or until the fish is crispy on both sides. Repeat with the other fillets, adding up to 1 Tbsp of oil to the pan before searing each one. (Don't worry if some of the fillets split slightly while you sear them. In fact, if the fillets split even a little, you will easily be able to tell if they are fully cooked through.) Place cooked fillets on a tray, a large plate or directly in the bowls you will serve them in.

TO SERVE Place 1 fillet in each of six large, shallow bowls. Gently pour piping hot chickpea and yam curry over the halibut. Be sure to be generous with the curry.

WINE We serve a Pacific Northwest Pinot Gris with some residual sugar.

CURRY

½ cup ghee (page 30)

1 Tbsp black mustard seeds

4 bunches green onions, white part only, thinly sliced (5 to 6 stalks per bunch)

2 jalapeño peppers, thinly sliced lengthwise

1 oz ginger, thinly sliced in slivers

¼ cup dry white wine

1½ Tbsp ground cumin

1 Tbsp salt

HALIBUT

1½ tsp salt

1½ tsp ground cayenne pepper

6 fillets Pacific halibut, each about 5 oz

⅓ to ½ cup canola oil for searing

PACIFIC HALIBUT
IN COCONUT CURRY

HALIBUT

½ cup canola oil

½ tsp ground
cayenne pepper

½ Tbsp salt

2 tsp ground black
mustard seeds

1 tsp dried green
fenugreek leaves

6 fillets Pacific halibut,
each about 7 oz

1 cup ground bread crumbs

⅓ to ½ cup canola
oil for searing

W**E ORIGINALLY USED** orange roughy in this recipe, but when we realized it is considered to be an endangered fish, we switched to halibut. Not a single customer missed the orange roughy. If you can't find Pacific halibut, substitute a similar firm white fish that is readily, and preferably locally, available.

You can use the coconut curry to make many different meals. It tastes great with prawns, grilled chicken or vegetables. It does not go well with red meats. Serve this dish with plain rice or naan.

Serves 6

HALIBUT Mix oil, cayenne, salt, mustard seeds and fenugreek in a large mixing bowl. Gently add fillets and mix well. Make sure halibut is well covered in the marinade. Cover the bowl with plastic wrap and refrigerate for at least 2 hours.

COCONUT CURRY Heat oil in a medium pot on medium heat for 1 minute. Add curry leaves and allow them to sizzle for about 45 seconds. (Keep your face at a distance, as water from within the leaves can sometimes splatter.) The leaves should shrivel a bit. Add garlic and sauté for 3 to 4 minutes, until light brown. Add onions and sauté until brown, about 10 minutes. Stir in tomatoes and cumin, coriander, salt, cayenne and cloves. Continue cooking for 8 minutes, or until the water from the tomatoes has evaporated and the oil glistens on top. Add water and coconut milk. Bring to a boil. Cover, reduce the heat and simmer for about 15 minutes.

FINISH HALIBUT Spread bread crumbs on a flat plate. Dip each fillet in bread crumbs, making sure both sides of each piece are completely coated. Arrange coated fillets on a baking tray.

Heat 1 Tbsp of the oil in a small nonstick frying pan on medium-high heat for 1 minute. Sear a breaded fillet on one side for 2 to 3 minutes. The bread crumbs will be darkish brown. Gently turn the fillet over and sear for another 2 to 3 minutes. Turn the fillet over again, and cook the first side for 2 more minutes. Turn the fillet once more and cook the second side for 1 to 2 minutes, or until the fillet is cooked through. Repeat with each remaining fillet, adding up to 1 Tbsp of oil per fillet. Place cooked fillets on a large plate or directly in the bowls you will serve them in. You don't want to place the cooked fillets on paper towels, as the bread crumbs will stick to the towels.

TO SERVE Place 1 fillet in each of six shallow bowls. Remember that this curry has cloves in it. Using a slotted spoon, take out and discard the cloves or warn your guests to expect cloves in the dish. Gently pour one-sixth of the hot coconut curry over each fillet.

WINE A Muscat Ottonel is delicious with this fish.

COCONUT CURRY

½ cup canola oil

20 to 25 curry leaves

3 Tbsp chopped garlic

1 cup puréed onions (1 large)

1 lb tomatoes, finely chopped (4 medium)

1 Tbsp ground cumin

1 Tbsp ground coriander

1 Tbsp + 1 tsp salt

½ tsp ground cayenne pepper

6 whole cloves

3 cups water

1 cup coconut milk, stirred

STURGEON, MUSSELS

AND BABY CARROTS IN TOMATO, LIGHT CREAM CURRY

2½ cups tomato broth (page 31)

4 cups water

1 oz ginger, in thin slivers

1 oz garlic, in thin slivers

1 small jalapeño pepper

1 Tbsp black mustard seeds

1 Tbsp salt

½ tsp turmeric

1 tsp paprika

1½-inch stick of cinnamon

½ to ¾ cup whipping cream

30 mussels

1 bunch small carrots (minimum of 6 carrots), washed, scrubbed and greens removed

1½ lbs sturgeon, in 2-inch × 3-inch pieces (3 to 4 oz per serving)

6 Tbsp fennel and Indian thyme–candied walnuts (page 190) (optional)

 HIS IS ONE of the few curries for which we don't first make a masala. Nothing is sautéed and very few spices are used. We serve this curry with Fennel- and Indian Thyme–candied Walnuts (page 190). Although it has the same basic ingredients as Grilled Sablefish in Tomato-Yogurt Broth (page 121), this dish tastes quite different.

Sturgeon is best known as the fish that has existed since the time of the dinosaurs. According to marine environmental groups, wild sturgeon is nearly extinct. The one exception is white sturgeon from the Columbia River in Oregon. Farmed sturgeon, however, is highly sustainable as a fishery, and we find the quality of the fish to be excellent. If you can't find any sturgeon, use halibut or any other firm, white fish.

Many supermarkets sell pre-washed and cleaned mussels. If you buy from a seafood or farmer's market, fresh mussels may need to be cleaned. Make sure to buy only fresh mussels whose shells are closed.

You will have to weigh the whole piece of ginger since it's difficult to measure the long, thin slivers necessary for this recipe. Be sure to use a large pot for the light cream curry, as you will need a lot of space once you add the seafood. Serve this dish with a bowl of rice.

Serves 6

COMBINE TOMATO broth, water, ginger, garlic, jalapeño pepper, mustard seeds, salt, turmeric, paprika and cinnamon in a large pot and stir well. Place on medium heat and bring to a boil. Reduce the heat to low, but not to a simmer. Cook curry, uncovered, for 45 minutes, stirring occasionally. As it cooks, the smell of the cinnamon should become stronger. Turn off the heat and allow curry to cool slightly, about 10 minutes.

Turn on the heat to medium and add ½ cup of the whipping cream. Taste a teaspoonful of the curry (be careful not to burn your tongue). If the curry seems too tart, add another ¼ cup whipping cream. This isn't meant to be a rich curry. Remove from the heat and set aside.

Wash mussels thoroughly and, with a paring knife, scrape off any grit and grime on the shells. Chop carrots in half or thirds.

Return curry to a boil on medium heat, then reduce heat to medium-low and add sturgeon. Stir gently and cook for 1 minute. Add mussels and carrots. Stir gently, cover and cook for 4 minutes. Immediately remove the lid and turn off the heat. The mussel shells should be open and the sturgeon should be firm and white.

TO SERVE Using a large ladle, divide equal portions of mussels, sturgeon, carrots and curry among six large shallow bowls. Sprinkle a tablespoon of candied walnuts over each serving (optional).

WINE A Condrieu from Côtes du Rhône goes very well with this Indian-style bouillabaisse.

GRILLED SABLEFISH

IN TOMATO-YOGURT BROTH

SABLEFISH IS A slightly oily fish that needs careful handling on the grill so it doesn't fall apart. The broth in this recipe is very light and delicate in flavour. We recommend that you use 4% milkfat yogurt, as it gives a smoother finish. Serve this dish with plain basmati rice. The broth does not go well with naan.

Serves 6

SABLEFISH Mix oil, cayenne, salt and paprika in a large mixing bowl. Gently add fish and mix well. Make sure the sablefish is well covered in the marinade. Cover the bowl with plastic wrap and refrigerate for 3 to 4 hours.

TOMATO-YOGURT BROTH In a mixing bowl, combine yogurt, garam masala, salt, paprika and cayenne. Set aside.

In a medium pot, heat oil on medium heat and sauté garlic until golden brown. Add ginger and sauté 1 more minute. Add tomato broth, then the yogurt mixture. Stir well, reduce the heat to low and simmer for 10 minutes.

FINISH SABLEFISH Preheat a barbeque or stovetop flat-iron grill to high heat. (If using the stovetop grill, turn on your exhaust fan.) Using metal tongs, carefully place marinated sablefish pieces on the grill and cook on one side for 2 minutes. Turn sablefish pieces over and grill for 2 minutes more. As the fish cooks, it will look less "fleshy." If the centre still looks raw, grill each side for another 30 seconds. You want to retain the oiliness of the fish, so be careful not to overcook it.

TO SERVE Divide sablefish evenly among six bowls, placing the fish in the centre. Pour hot broth around the sablefish. Serve immediately.

WINE The bubbles from a champagne or sparkling wine pair nicely with the tomato-yogurt broth.

SABLEFISH

½ cup canola oil

¼ tsp ground cayenne pepper

½ tsp salt

½ tsp paprika

1 lb 5 oz sablefish, in 2-inch × 3-inch pieces

TOMATO-YOGURT BROTH

1 cup plain yogurt, stirred (4% milkfat recommended)

1½ Tbsp garam masala (page 26)

½ Tbsp salt

2 tsp paprika

½ tsp ground cayenne pepper

¼ cup canola oil

2½ Tbsp chopped garlic

3 Tbsp finely chopped ginger

2½ cups tomato broth, heated (page 31)

PANFRIED SALMON POTATO CAKES

1 Tbsp coriander seeds

1 egg

1 lb fresh or tinned
wild salmon

a little over ½ lb russet
potatoes, boiled and
mashed (about 1 potato)

¼ lb boiled yams, mashed
(about 1 yam)

3 Tbsp all-purpose flour

⅓ cup finely chopped onions

1 Tbsp finely chopped
jalapeño peppers

¼ to ½ cup
chopped cilantro

1½ Tbsp garam masala
(page 26) or 1 Tbsp
ground cumin

½ tsp ajwain seeds

1 Tbsp salt

½ cup canola oil
for pan frying

LTHOUGH THERE ARE many ways to cook fish curries, we find the flavour of salmon just isn't right for curries. However, salmon is perfect for grilling on skewers or, in this case, for making fish cakes. We use only wild salmon at Vij's. If you are unable to buy fresh, wild salmon, you can also use tinned salmon packed in water. Just remember to squeeze out the water before you add the salmon to the other ingredients. Tinned salmon is always wild and is actually very nutritious.

At home, Meeru makes a milder version of these cakes for our daughters. If you want to make these cakes less spicy, don't add any jalapeño peppers. You can also take out the ajwain seed, but it adds a nice flavour and most children don't seem to mind it.

Once you get the hang of this recipe, you can add an additional vegetable such as chopped spinach or peas. If you don't have any garam masala, you can substitute ground cumin; we just prefer the different layers of spicing the garam masala gives to the cakes. Serve these cakes on their own as an appetizer with chutney or as a main course with Creamy Bengali-style Curry (page 64) and rice or naan.

Serves 6 (about 24 to 28 cakes)

LIGHTLY POUND coriander seeds in a mortar or on a plate with a heavy spoon. (You just want to break the seeds in half.) Set aside.

Beat egg in a small bowl.

If you are using fresh salmon, bring a large pot of water to a boil. Immerse salmon and cook for 5 minutes. Remove from the heat, drain and allow salmon to cool. Peel off the skin.

Thoroughly combine all ingredients except the oil in a large mixing bowl. With your hands, form round cakes about 2 inches in diameter and 1 inch thick. Set them on a baking tray.

Heat 1 Tbsp of the oil in a shallow nonstick frying pan on high heat. Once the oil is hot, reduce the heat to medium so the cakes don't stick to the bottom of the pan or burn. Place 2 cakes in the pan and cook for 2 to 3 minutes. Turn cakes over and cook for another 2 to 3 minutes. The cakes should be brown and crispy on both sides. Repeat, using 1 Tbsp of oil for each 2 cakes, until all the cakes are cooked. Serve cakes as they cook or keep cooked cakes warm on a plate in the oven while the remaining ones are cooking.

TO SERVE There are many ways to serve these cakes. If serving as an informal appetizer, you can place them on a large platter with chutneys on the side. If serving casually, just place them on dinner plates as they come out of the frying pan—just be sure to keep chutneys on the table. As a formal appetizer or main course, arrange 4 to 5 cakes on a plate with chutneys, or with naan and rice and the creamy Bengali-style curry in side bowls.

WINE Try Nero d'Avola from Sicily, which is great with the spiced salmon.

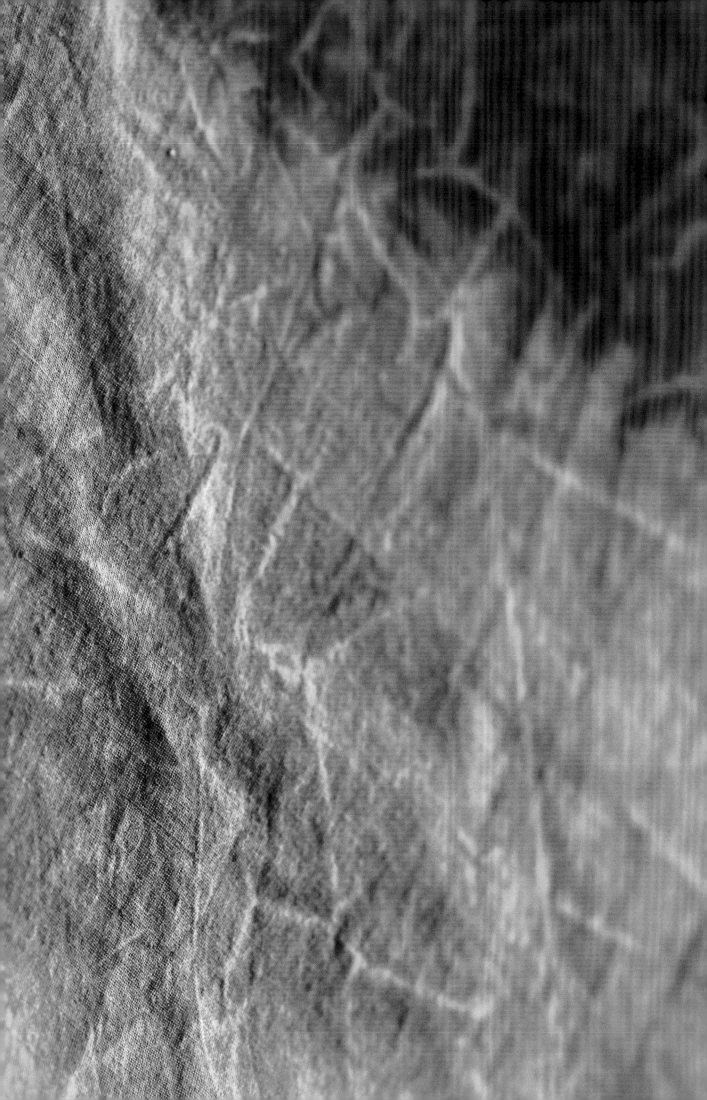

MAINS

Vegetables

GRILLED CORN
WITH LEMON/LIME RUB

6 ears corn, husked
but stems attached

1½ Tbsp salt or black salt

1 tsp ground cayenne pepper

1½ tsp mango powder
(use this only with
the regular salt)

1½ lemons or limes

ONE OF MEERU'S fondest memories of India is watching a crowd of people eating grilled corn by the side of a dirt road near a Himalayan hill station. A man was quickly dabbing half a lime in a mixture of black salt, red and black peppers then rubbing it on a cob of corn that had just been grilled to perfection. On a makeshift barbeque, the man quickly fanned the coals with a piece of torn cardboard, grilling the next few ears of corn. A large group of people formed around him, some already eating, others awaiting this delicious, hot grilled corn. The sun was setting and the evening chill had begun, and the scene was mesmerizing: it was food and ambience in their most natural state.

We can't recreate the exact atmosphere of the Himalayas, but you can still enjoy this flavourful, simple dish when corn is in season. Serve it during the summer, at an evening barbeque. If you don't have a barbeque, use a stovetop grill, as we did when we lived in an apartment and used to eat dinner at midnight on our small balcony.

Try making the rub with the black salt. It is available at most Indian grocers. If you don't have black salt, use regular salt and combine it with mango powder to create the correct tartness. If you have neither black salt nor mango powder, just rub the corn with regular salt and the cayenne pepper. You will almost always make more of the rub than you need.

It doesn't matter whether you use lemons or limes in this recipe—just choose the juicier of the two fruit. You must rub the lemon (or lime) and the spices onto a piping hot cob of corn, so grill the corn one or two at a time. You may wish to have toothpicks on hand, as you will most certainly get small dark pieces of corn stuck in your teeth!

Serves 6

PREHEAT A BARBEQUE or stovetop cast-iron grill to medium-high. Combine salt (or black salt), cayenne and mango powder (if using regular salt) in a bowl.

Cut the whole lemon (or lime) in half. Rub the cut halves into the spice mixture, coating them well. Set aside with a small tea towel by the barbeque (or grill).

Using metal tongs, set 2 cobs corn directly on the barbeque (or grill). As with popcorn, you will hear kernels popping, just not as often. Keep your face away from the corn, as hot juices from the kernels sometimes pop out as well. Cook corn, turning it frequently so it grills uniformly, for 8 to 10 minutes. Some kernels will be dark brown, others will be light brown and a few will still be dark yellow. This means that the corn has grilled perfectly.

Using tongs, immediately remove corn from the heat. Place the tea towel in the palm of your free hand, then with that hand, grab the corn cob by its stem. Rub spice-dabbed lemon (or lime) over hot corn. Use half a lemon (or lime) per two cobs of corn. Squeeze the lemon (or lime) only very gently as you rub, so the flavour does not become too sour. Repeat with the remaining cobs, cutting and dabbing the remaining lemons (or limes) as you cook the corn.

TO SERVE Serve immediately, providing napkins and toothpicks.

WINE This is another sparkling water dish. The corn and tartness just don't go well with wines.

GRILLED ASPARAGUS
AND CORN IN FENUGREEK SEED CURRY

T HIS RECIPE IS very simple, and only simple ingredients taste good with it. We don't even use a stock of any kind because we want just the flavours of the garlic, ginger and fenugreek seeds. You will taste this curry and still wonder what exactly fenugreek seeds taste like, but they're there. It's difficult to pinpoint the flavour of the perfect amount of fenugreek seeds, but measure carefully because even a tad too much can make your entire curry bitter. Note that ground fenugreek seeds can burn easily if you add them alone to hot oil.

We use asparagus and corn when they are in season. Although the season for asparagus tends to be May and June in some places, you can generally buy it throughout the summer. And since they are in season during the summer months, we usually grill or barbeque them. If you don't have a grill, steam the corn and lightly panfry the asparagus—just make sure they retain their crunch. We have given instructions for both grilling and panfrying. Remember that asparagus cooks very quickly and isn't as delicious if it overcooks. You can also use zucchini and bell peppers, if you prefer.

Because this dish isn't very spicy, you can also serve it on its own as an appetizer without any naan or rice.

Serves 6

FENUGREEK SEED CURRY

½ cup canola oil

3 Tbsp finely chopped garlic

2 Tbsp finely chopped ginger

1 cup ground tomatoes
(canned works best)

1 tsp ground
fenugreek seeds

1 tsp salt

½ tsp ground
cayenne pepper

2 cups water

FENUGREEK SEED CURRY Heat oil in a pan on medium heat for 1 minute. Stir in garlic and sauté for 3 to 4 minutes, until slightly golden. You will have to stir vigorously so the garlic doesn't stick and burn to the bottom. Stir in ginger and sauté for another 4 to 5 minutes. Turn off the heat.

Add ground tomatoes and stir. Add fenugreek, salt and cayenne, and turn on the heat to medium. Stir again and cook for 4 to 5 minutes, until the top glistens with oil. Add water, stir and bring to a boil. Reduce the heat to low and simmer for 5 minutes. Turn off the heat.

ASPARAGUS AND CORN

3 cobs of corn, husked

15 oz asparagus
(about 30 stalks)

1 Tbsp canola oil

½ tsp salt

GRILLING THE ASPARAGUS AND CORN Preheat a grill or barbeque to high heat. Using metal tongs, place corn cobs directly on the hot grill (or barbeque). Keep your face away from the corn, as kernels and hot juices from the kernels sometimes pop out. Cook corn, turning it frequently so it grills uniformly, for 8 to 10 minutes. Some kernels will be dark brown, others will be light brown and a few will still be dark yellow. This means that the corn has grilled perfectly.

Cool corn for 10 minutes, or until cobs are warm but no longer hot. Using a sharp knife, shave kernels off the cob.

Remove and discard the tough lower part of the asparagus stalks. Wash asparagus and air dry in a colander.

Combine asparagus, oil and salt in a large bowl. Mix well. Using tongs, place each asparagus stalk individually on the hot grill or barbeque. Grill asparagus, turning every 15 to 30 seconds, for 2 minutes. The asparagus should be brown at the edges and lightly crispy.

PANFRYING THE ASPARAGUS AND STEAMING THE CORN Place corn cobs in 1 inch of water in a shallow pan. Bring water to a boil on high heat, then reduce to low. Cover and cook corn for 5 minutes. Cool cobs for 10 minutes, or submerge in a bowl of cold water for 20 seconds. (Do not submerge grilled corn as a way to cool it quickly.)

Using a sharp knife, shave kernels off the cob.

Remove and discard the tough lower part of the asparagus stalks. Wash asparagus and air dry in a colander.

Heat oil in a heavy frying pan on high heat for 1 minute. Add asparagus and salt and cook for 2 to 3 minutes, stirring regularly. Reduce the heat to medium if asparagus starts to burn.

TO SERVE In shallow bowls, divide the asparagus and corn into six servings. Reheat the fenugreek seed curry, if necessary. Pour piping hot curry over the vegetables and serve.

WINE A dry, crisp Soave Superiore is a perfect match.

EGGPLANT, TOMATO
AND GREEN ONION CURRY

THIS IS A very easy recipe that cooks quickly. The green onions and the yogurt are the predominant flavours. You can't really go overboard on the onions, so it doesn't matter if you use a little more than what is written, but follow the measurement for the yogurt, as too much will overtake the other spices and make this dish too tangy. The white parts of the green onions have a different flavour and texture than the green parts, so each should be chopped in different sizes.

It is important to use a large meaty purple eggplant rather than a Japanese eggplant. When buying eggplant, compare eggplants of the same size and choose the ones that weigh less. This has been the tradition for generations in both our families, as this apparently increases the chances of getting eggplants with more meat and fewer seeds. This doesn't affect the flavour, but some people find the seeds irritating. Serve this curry with chapattis and/or raita (page 156).

Serves 6

7 oz green onions (about 8 stalks)

1 cup plain yogurt, stirred

1 Tbsp Mexican chili powder

1 tsp turmeric

1 tsp ground cayenne pepper

2½ tsp salt

1 eggplant, skin on, in 1-inch cubes

2 cups chopped tomatoes (2 large)

½ cup canola oil

WASH GREEN ONIONS. Chop white parts in rounds ¼ inch long. Remove and discard the hollow green parts. Chop the remaining green parts in rounds ¾ inch long. Set aside.

In a large mixing bowl, combine yogurt, chili powder, turmeric, cayenne and salt. Add eggplant, tomatoes and onions and stir well to make sure vegetables are well covered in the curry mixture.

In a shallow heavy pan, heat oil on medium-high heat for 45 seconds. Pour curry into the pan and stir well. Sauté for about 3 minutes, reduce the heat to medium-low and cover. Simmer for another 10 minutes, stirring once halfway through the cooking. Turn off the heat and stir once more. Remove the lid if you are not going to serve the curry immediately, or the eggplant will become too mushy.

TO SERVE Ladle curry into six bowls or plates. If serving with another curry, serve this one in a bowl, so that it doesn't "run" on the plate.

WINE We drink a California Barbera to go with the spicy onions.

JAPANESE EGGPLANT

WITH TAMARIND AND KALONJI CURRY AND COUSCOUS

JAPANESE EGGPLANT

1½ lbs Japanese eggplants, skin on (about 3 large)

¼ cup canola oil

1 tsp salt

....

TAMARIND AND KALONJI CURRY

⅓ cup canola oil

1 tsp kalonji

1 Tbsp cumin seeds

1½ cups finely chopped onions (1 large)

2 cups chopped tomatoes (4 medium)

½ tsp black cardamom seeds (discard the pods)

½ tsp ground cayenne pepper

1 tsp ground coriander

1 Tbsp salt

2 Tbsp tamarind paste (page 32)

1 Tbsp sugar (any kind)

2 cups water

....

3 cups freshly cooked couscous

 HIS IS ONE of our original recipes from ten years ago. It is a hearty appetizer or a light meal, but since it has very strong flavours it doesn't work well as a side dish. At the restaurant, we grill the eggplant but it also tastes great baked in the oven. The kalonji gives this curry a bit of bitterness, the tamarind gives it a tartness and the sugar gives it a slight sweetness. If you don't like things tart, then decrease the tamarind by half. The eggplant soaks in all three flavours beautifully. This same curry will not taste as good with a less meaty vegetable such as cauliflower but if you don't like eggplant, you can use zucchini.

You can buy couscous at any grocery store and prepare it according to the instructions on the package for 6 servings. It's best to make the couscous just prior to serving, as it can get clumpy if it sits out too long or is stored in the refrigerator.

Serves 6

....

JAPANESE EGGPLANT Preheat the oven to 375°F. Cut eggplants in 3 round pieces, then slice each round in quarters. Rub the eggplant slices with oil and salt them lightly. Place the slices in a single layer on a baking tray. Bake for 15 minutes and set aside. Do not refrigerate cooked eggplant, as it becomes soggy when reheated on the stove, or dry if reheated in the oven.

TAMARIND AND KALONJI CURRY Heat oil in a medium pot on medium-high heat for 1 minute. Add kalonji, then 15 seconds later add cumin seeds, stir and allow seeds to sizzle for 45 seconds. Add onions and sauté for about 10 minutes, until brown. Stir in tomatoes and add black cardamom, cayenne, coriander and salt. Cook the masala for about 5 minutes, or until the oil glistens through the tomatoes. Add tamarind and sugar, stirring well. Cook the masala for 1 to 2 minutes more. Stir in water, bring to a boil, cover and simmer for 5 minutes.

TO SERVE Arrange ½ cup of hot couscous on each of six individual plates. Place 4 to 5 slices of eggplant on top. Ladle the hot tamarind and kalonji curry over the eggplant.

WINE If you can get your hands on a bottle (and chances are you just might), try a sparkling wine from India. If not, drink a lighter sparkling wine from the Loire Valley in France.

EGGPLANT AND PAPAYA
CURRY WITH BLACK CHICKPEAS

W E COMBINE ROASTED eggplant and papaya with Black Chickpea Curry (page 143). Do not buy fully ripened, soft papayas, as they become very difficult to handle and they are too sweet. This dish will *not* taste as good without the black chickpea curry added to it. The black chickpea curry has many of its own spices, so we've used much less spicing in this eggplant-papaya curry.

If you have a grill or a barbeque, you can reduce the roasting time by more than half. Just place each eggplant and papaya on a fully heated grill or barbeque. Allow the papaya to cook through for about 15 minutes and the eggplants for 20 to 25 minutes, while turning them regularly. Don't worry that the skin of the eggplant or papaya will have some burn marks on it. These marks will actually give them a roasted flavour.

At their home, Vikram's mother and father dry fresh mint leaves for Vij's, as the restaurant doesn't get enough direct sunlight for drying the mint leaves properly. It's a fairly long process, depending on the amount of sun. Store-bought dried mint leaves aren't as *minty* and don't taste as fresh, but if you like mint, we recommend you buy the dried leaves, rub them between your hands and sprinkle them on this curry just before serving. Serve this dish with chapattis, lentil chapattis (page 176) or naan.

Serves 6 to 8

2 medium eggplants (about 2 lbs)

3 medium to large semi-ripe papayas (about 2¼ lbs)

½ cup canola oil

2 very large onions, in 1½-inch dice (about 1½ lbs)

3 large ripened tomatoes, in 1½-inch dice (1 lb)

1½ Tbsp ground cumin

½ tsp turmeric

1 tsp ground fenugreek seeds

1 large jalapeño pepper, chopped

1½ Tbsp salt

2 cups black chickpea curry (page 143)

1 cup chopped cilantro

1½ tsp dried mint leaves (optional)

PREHEAT THE OVEN to 450°F. Wrap eggplants and papayas individually in aluminum foil. Place them on a baking tray. Since the papayas will cook faster, place them in the front so you can easily remove them from the oven. Bake papayas for 30 minutes, then remove from the oven and allow them to cool. Continue baking eggplants for 1 hour more, or until they are very soft. The eggplants will become mushy and deflated. Remove eggplants from the oven and cool so you can unwrap the aluminum foil.

Using a paring knife or a potato peeler, peel papayas and discard the skin. Cut papayas in half. Using a spoon, scoop out seeds and discard. Purée papaya flesh in a food processor or finely mash papayas with your hands.

Using a paring knife, peel skins off eggplant. Using a spoon, scrape off any eggplant stuck to the skins. Discard the skins. Coarsely chop eggplant into a mixing bowl, then using your hands, roughly mash the eggplants. They will have nowhere near the smooth consistency of mashed potatoes; instead, there will be some chunks. (You can also place the whole eggplants on a large cutting board and dice them in ¼- to ½-inch pieces with a knife.)

Add the papaya purée to the eggplants and mix well. Set aside.

Heat oil in a large heavy frying pan on medium-high heat for 1 minute. Add onions and sauté until brown, about 15 minutes. Reduce the heat to medium and stir in tomatoes. Add cumin, turmeric, fenugreek, jalapeño pepper and salt. Cook for 10 minutes. Pour the eggplant and papaya mixture into the masala and stir well. Combine the eggplant and papaya curry with the black chickpea curry and heat on medium for 5 to 10 minutes, or until the mixture is gently boiling. Stir in the chopped cilantro just as you turn off the heat.

TO SERVE Serve this curry on six plates with chapattis or lentil chapattis. Sprinkle dried mint on top of the curry on each plate.

WINE Choose a cool-climate Pinot Blanc, as it has good acidity that complements this curry.

OVEN-ROASTED EGGPLANT

AND BUTTERNUT SQUASH CURRY

3 medium eggplants,
total weight 3½ lbs

1½ lbs butternut squash

½ cup canola oil

½ tsp asafoetida

1½ Tbsp cumin seeds

3 medium-large onions, in
1½-inch dice (about 1½ lbs)

3 large ripened tomatoes, in
1½-inch dice (about 1 lb)

½ tsp turmeric

1 tsp ground fenugreek seeds

1 Tbsp ground coriander

½ tsp ground black pepper

1 large jalapeño pepper,
chopped

1½ Tbsp salt

1 bunch green onions
(5 or 6 stalks),
in 1-inch pieces

1 cup chopped cilantro

 P TO A POINT, this recipe is similar to the eggplant and papaya curry. The end product, however, tastes very different. If you have a grill or a barbeque, you can reduce the baking time of the eggplants and squash by more than half. Just place each eggplant and the butternut squash on a fully heated grill or barbeque and allow them to cook through for about 20 to 25 minutes, while turning the eggplant regularly; the squash doesn't need to be turned. Don't worry about burn marks on either vegetable.

This recipe has lots of onions in it, and since they are chopped in large pieces, it's difficult to measure them in cups. So don't worry about being precise with the weights. We want the onions to be browned on the outside and soft on the inside, so we sauté them on high heat. The tomatoes are also chopped in large pieces, so the same goes for measuring them.

Serve with a thin bread such as chapattis or lentil chapattis (page 176). *Serves 6*

PREHEAT THE OVEN to 450°F. Wrap eggplants and squash individually in aluminum foil. Place them on a baking tray and bake them for 1½ hours or until they are very soft. The eggplants will become mushy and deflated.

While the eggplants and squash are cooking, heat oil in a large heavy frying pan on medium-high heat for 1 minute. Sprinkle in asafoetida and cook for 20 seconds, or just until its colour slightly darkens. Add cumin seeds and allow them to sizzle for about 30 seconds. Stir in onions and sauté until brown, 8 to 10 minutes. Reduce the heat to medium and stir in the tomatoes. Add turmeric, fenugreek, coriander, black pepper, jalapeño pepper and salt. Cook this masala for 10 minutes. If the eggplants and squash are still cooking, remove the masala from the heat and set aside.

Remove eggplants and squash from the oven and cool for 5 to 10 minutes so you can unwrap the aluminum foil.

Using a paring knife or a potato peeler, peel squash and discard the skin. Cut squash in half. Using a spoon, scoop out the seeds from the squash and discard. Place flesh in a large mixing bowl.

Using your hands, peel skin from eggplants. Using a spoon, scrape off any eggplant stuck to the skins. Discard the skins. Add eggplants to the mixing bowl. Using your hands, roughly mash the squash and eggplants. They will have nowhere near the smooth consistency of mashed potatoes; instead, there will be some chunks. (You can also place the whole squash and eggplants on a large cutting board and dice them into ¼- to ½-inch pieces with a knife.)

Stir the eggplant and squash mixture into the masala. Turn the heat on to medium and cook, covered, for 10 minutes. Just before serving, stir in green onions and heat for 2 to 3 minutes. Do not overcook the green onions. Remove from the heat and stir in cilantro.

TO SERVE Serve this curry on six individual plates with chapattis or lentil chapattis. This dish can also go directly on individual plates along with other meat or poultry curries.

WINE We suggest a Riesling vendange tardive (late harvest) from Alsace.

BITTER MELON

WITH PANEER AND RAW SUGAR

IT TOOK US years to work up the courage to put bitter melon (also known as bitter gourd) on the menu because we were worried that non-Asian palates would find it too bitter or just plain weird. In our families, it was a delicacy for many of us (but not all). Bitter melon is highly regarded in India for its health benefits, and the joke goes that something so healthy could only be bitter. Indians believe that it "cleans the blood" of any impurities. One of our cook's mothers has diabetes and eats bitter melon regularly to keep her blood sugar level low, and we are all convinced that it works.

In Singapore, Meeru noticed many people in the food courts eating a tofu and bitter melon soup for lunch. She ordered it and decided quickly that it was an acquired taste, even though it wasn't nearly as bitter as Indian bitter melon. There was no spicing in the soup—it was stock, boiled bitter melon and plain tofu. Later, she found out that the soup was eaten more for its internal cleansing properties and health benefits than for its taste.

When we finally came up with a recipe that kept the bitter as mild as possible while highlighting the flavours, we asked our vegetable supplier if he could procure a regular supply. He is Chinese and burst into a huge smile, telling Meeru that "bitter gourd is my favourite vegetable and I'm so happy that you are going to start making it." Now, we want to encourage non-Asians to try bitter melon. When prepared properly, it is one of the most different-tasting and delicious vegetables. We have chosen to use Chinese bitter melons, as they are milder and available for most of the year. You can buy them at many Asian grocers. Since we add the spices after the vegetable is cooked, it's important to use roasted, ground cumin and coriander (page 29). At Vij's we serve this dish with Tamarind-marinated Chicken Breast in Coconut–Chickpea Flour Curry (page 96) but it can also be eaten with chapattis as part of a vegetarian meal.

If you are making this dish ahead of time, add the red bell peppers only when you reheat this dish. They become quite mushy and lose their flavour if they get overcooked.

Serves 6

PEEL THE SHINY skin off the bitter melons with a peeler. Cut off both ends of the melon, like you would for a cucumber. Cut bitter melons in half lengthwise. Using a spoon, scrape out and discard thick seeds and fibres. Cut each half lengthwise in quarters. Cut these quarters in ½-inch slices.

Heat oil in a medium pot on medium heat for 1 minute. Add onions and sauté for 5 to 8 minutes, or until golden brown. Reduce the heat to low, add bitter melon, then cook and stir for 8 minutes. You will notice that the bitter melon has gone from jade green to light tan. Stir in raw sugar. Cook and stir raw sugar and melon for 5 minutes, until the sugar has completely melted and mixed in.

Add cumin, coriander, salt and cayenne and stir well. Cook for 3 to 4 minutes, then add paneer and buttermilk. Stir again and cook for 5 minutes. Stir in bell peppers, cook for 1 minute and turn off the heat.

TO SERVE Divide equal portions of curry among six bowls or plates and serve with chapatti. If you are serving this dish with the tamarind-marinated chicken breast, serve the bitter melon over the chicken and pour the coconut–chickpea flour curry around the chicken.

WINE We are hard pressed to find a wine that would go nicely with this dish on its own. If you are serving this dish with another vegetarian or meat entrée, drink the wine recommended for that entrée. Otherwise, enjoy it with a ginger-lemon drink (page 194).

just less than 1 lb Chinese bitter melons (2 large)

½ cup canola oil

3 cups finely chopped onions (3 medium)

2 Tbsp crushed raw sugar

½ Tbsp ground cumin

1 Tbsp ground coriander

1 Tbsp salt

½ tsp ground cayenne pepper

1 lb paneer (page 34), in ½-inch cubes

¾ cup buttermilk

1 large red bell pepper, in ½-inch cubes

LONG GREEN BEANS

AND NEW POTATOES IN MUSTARD SEED CURRY

9 oz new potatoes

½ cup canola oil

1½ Tbsp cumin seeds

3 cups puréed
tomatoes (6 large)

1 Tbsp ground
black mustard seeds

1 Tbsp salt

1 Tbsp crushed
cayenne pepper

1 tsp turmeric

4⅓ cups water

9 oz green beans,
strings removed,
cut in half lengthwise

 THIS IS A slightly tart curry with lots of tomatoes. You can also add or substitute other vegetables, but it's important to keep the potatoes. And we don't recommend eggplant, as it doesn't taste good with this particular spicing. Remember that different vegetables have different cooking times and you will have to add them to the curry accordingly. At Vij's we serve this dish with the Brown Rice and French Green Lentil Pilaf (page 169) for a richer flavour but you can serve it with any rice, including plain rice if you prefer a milder taste.

Serves 6

SOAK NEW POTATOES in water for 10 minutes to loosen any dirt. Drain and thoroughly wash the potatoes, then cut each one in 4 to 6 slices. Set aside.

In a medium pot, heat oil on high for 1 minute. Sprinkle in cumin seeds, stir and allow to sizzle for about 30 seconds. Reduce the heat to medium and add tomatoes, mustard seeds, salt, cayenne and turmeric. Stir well and cook this masala for 5 to 8 minutes, or until oil glistens on top. Stir in water and bring to boil on medium-high heat for 8 to 10 minutes, stirring occasionally. If the curry still seems very runny and watery, boil for another 5 minutes. The spices and the water should be very well mixed together at the end of boiling.

Turn down the heat to medium-low. Add potatoes and cook at a medium boil, covered, for 5 to 8 minutes. Add green beans, stir well, and cook, uncovered, for 5 minutes.

TO SERVE Serve piping hot in six individual bowls.

WINE An aromatic Alsatian Gewurztraminer balances the heat of this dish beautifully.

COCONUT CURRIED VEGETABLES

½ cup canola oil

25 to 30 fresh curry leaves

1 Tbsp black mustard seeds

1½ cups finely chopped onions (2 medium)

1 Tbsp + 1 tsp chopped garlic

2 cups chopped tomatoes (2 large)

1 Tbsp ground cumin

1 tsp turmeric

½ tsp ground cayenne pepper

1 Tbsp salt

½ tsp ground black pepper

1 (12 oz) can coconut milk, stirred

1 lb eggplant, in 1½-inch cubes

1 lb cauliflower, in 1½-inch florets

¾ lb red, green and/or yellow bell peppers, in 1½-inch cubes

¾ cup chopped cilantro

3 to 4 cups cooked basmati rice

 THIS IS A great vegetarian entrée, as it's rich in spices and you can use whichever vegetables you like. Just remember to add the vegetables according to how much time they take to cook; otherwise, you may end up with a vegetarian mush. You can even add firm tofu cut in cubes.

We've specified a 12-ounce can of coconut milk but, since each manufacturer's measurement varies by 1 or 2 ounces, don't worry too much about being precise. You just need one regular-size can. Serve with rice.

Serves 6 to 8

IN A LARGE POT, heat oil on medium heat for 1 minute. Keeping your head at a distance from the pot, add curry leaves and mustard seeds and allow them to sizzle for about 1 minute, or until just a few mustards seeds start to pop. (The curry leaves will cook and become shrivelled.) Immediately add onions and sauté until golden brown, about 8 minutes. Add garlic and sauté for 2 minutes. Add tomatoes and cumin, turmeric, cayenne, salt and black pepper. Sauté the masala for 5 to 8 minutes, or until the oil glistens on top. Stir in coconut milk. Bring to a boil and reduce the heat to medium-low. Add eggplant, cover and simmer for 5 minutes. Add cauliflower and bell peppers, cover and cook for 5 minutes more. Stir in cilantro.

TO SERVE Place ½ cup of hot rice in each of six to eight large bowls. Ladle curry over the rice.

WINE An aromatic Moscato d'Asti is perfect with the coconut and the vegetables.

BLACK CHICKPEA CURRY

HIS IS A family recipe that we incorporated into the Eggplant and Papaya Curry on page 133. At home we serve this curry as a main dish with side dishes of vegetables, rice and raita (page 156). If you are making this curry to go with the Eggplant and Papaya Curry, boil the chickpeas in 6½ rather than 9 cups of water. You can freeze any leftover curry in a sealed container; it will keep for up to 3 months.

Serves 4 on its own or 6 as an accompaniment

CHICKPEAS Wash and drain black chickpeas. Place chickpeas and the 3 cups of water in a bowl and soak overnight, or for at least 6 hours. Note that black chickpeas don't expand in size the way other beans do after soaking.

Drain chickpeas. Place chickpeas in a large pot with salt and the 9 cups of water. Bring to a boil on high heat, then reduce the heat to low, cover the pan and simmer for 1 hour or until chickpeas are cooked through. The outer skin of black chickpeas is thicker than the skin of regular yellow chickpeas, so taste one or mash one between your fingers to be sure they are fully cooked. Do not drain.

MASALA In a separate large pot, heat ghee on medium-high for 1 minute. Add cumin seeds and allow them to sizzle for about 30 seconds. Add onions and sauté for 8 minutes, stirring regularly, until golden brown. Add garlic and sauté for 2 to 3 minutes. Stir in tomatoes, then add jalapeño pepper, garam masala, mango powder, turmeric, fenugreek, salt and cayenne. Reduce the heat to medium and cook the masala for 5 to 8 minutes, until ghee glistens on top. Stir in water.

Add boiled chickpeas and their water to the masala. Bring to a boil on medium-high heat, then cover, reduce the heat to low and simmer for 10 to 15 minutes. (This ensures that the spicing has gone into the chickpeas.) Stir in cilantro.

TO SERVE Ladle curry into individual bowls. Serve immediately.

WINE An easy-drinking Primitivo is best with this curry.

CHICKPEAS

1 cup dried black chickpeas

3 cups water for soaking

½ tsp salt

9 cups water for boiling

MASALA

½ cup ghee (page 30)

1½ Tbsp cumin seeds

1 lb onions, chopped (2 medium)

2 Tbsp finely chopped garlic

1 large juicy tomato, finely chopped

1 large jalapeño pepper, finely chopped

1 Tbsp garam masala (page 26)

½ Tbsp mango powder

1 tsp turmeric

1 tsp ground fenugreek seeds

½ Tbsp salt

½ tsp ground cayenne pepper

2 cups water

½ cup chopped cilantro

SAVOURY RAW JACKFRUIT

3 cans (each 20 oz) young
(or raw) green jackfruit

6 black cardamom pods

½ cup canola oil

½ Tbsp cumin seeds

1 cup finely chopped
onions (1 large)

1 Tbsp finely chopped garlic

6 to 8 large whole
dried red chilies, broken in
half, with seeds

2 cups crushed tomatoes

½ Tbsp ground black
mustard seeds

1 tsp ground
fenugreek seeds

1 tsp turmeric

1 tsp Mexican chili powder

1 tsp paprika

1 tsp ground cumin

½ Tbsp ground coriander

1 Tbsp salt

1 cup water

6 cups oil for deep frying

R AW JACKFRUIT IS cooked and eaten as part of a vegetarian meal, whereas ripened, sweet jackfruit is eaten as a fruit with dessert. In North America, it is very difficult to buy fresh jackfruit, so we use canned; there isn't a drastic taste difference. It is available at all Indian or Asian grocers. Fresh jackfruit is white on the inside, with a thick green spiky skin. Make sure you drain the canned jackfruit fully before frying it, otherwise the water from it will splatter. The crushed tomatoes must also be very ripe. Canned, crushed tomatoes are preferable to light red, hard fresh tomatoes.

You must deep-fry the jackfruit lightly, otherwise it will have a funny chewy texture and won't hold well with all the spices and tomatoes. Note that if you have never deep-fried food before, this is not a good recipe to start with.

This recipe has been on our menu for years—we've taken it off, only to bring it back due to so many requests from customers. Although the black cardamom seeds, ground mustard seeds and ground fenugreek seeds give this dish its special Vij's flavour, you can make it without these 3 spices and still enjoy it, albeit with less depth of flavour. This is a heavily spiced dish that doesn't go very well with other heavily spiced meats, chicken or seafood. Serve it with chapattis, lentil chapattis (page 176) or naan.

Serves 6

LINE 2 BAKING TRAYS with clean, dry tea towels. Drain canned jackfruit and lay out pieces in a single layer on the tea towels to absorb any excess water. Set aside for about half an hour. (If you leave it out too long, the jackfruit will become too dry.)

Break open cardamom pods and remove the seeds. Discard the pods. Set aside the seeds.

Heat oil in a pan on medium-high heat for about 1 minute. Add cumin seeds and cook for about 30 seconds or until they begin to sizzle. Add onions and sauté 8 to 10 minutes, or until brown. Add garlic and dried chilies, including their seeds, and sauté for about 2 minutes. Stir in tomatoes and add cardamom seeds, mustard seeds, fenugreek, turmeric, chili powder, paprika, ground cumin, coriander and salt. Stir well and reduce the heat to medium.

Cook this masala, stirring regularly, for about 10 minutes or until the oil separates from the tomatoes and the masala glistens. Stir in water, turn off the heat and set aside.

Line a baking tray with paper towels. Preheat a deep fryer to high heat or heat oil in a large heavy pan on high heat for 5 minutes. Drop a small piece of jackfruit into the oil. It should immediately float to the top and sizzle. Once the oil is hot enough, place jackfruit in the pan and fry for about 5 minutes, or until very light brown. Keep your face at a distance, as the jackfruit can spatter a bit. Using tongs, transfer fried jackfruit to the paper towels to drain any excess oil. Turn off the deep fryer. Cool jackfruit for 15 minutes.

Carefully stir jackfruit into the masala so the pieces don't break, then turn the heat on to medium. Once the masala starts to boil and the jackfruit is well mixed into the spices, reduce the heat to medium-low, cover and simmer for 5 minutes. Remove the lid after 5 minutes so the jackfruit does not overcook.

TO SERVE Spoon piping hot jackfruit curry onto six plates.

WINE We recommend a Super Tuscan to go with the strong flavours.

GREEN ONION

AND COCONUT CHICKPEA CURRY

THIS IS ONE of the easiest recipes in this book. For convenience, we have used canned chickpeas, but you can soak and boil dried chickpeas if you prefer. Just be sure to drain and rinse the chickpeas well before you add them to the recipe.

This curry goes well with Grilled Coconut Kale (page 162) and/or naan. Although this dish has the zing of jalapeño peppers, it is very lightly spiced.

Serves 6

HEAT OIL in a medium pot on medium-high heat for 1 minute. Add cumin seeds and allow to sizzle for about 30 seconds. Add onions and sauté 8 to 10 minutes, or until they are brown. Stir in tomatoes, salt, ginger and jalapeño peppers and stir well. Sauté for about 5 to 8 minutes, or until oil glistens on top. Stir in chickpeas and coconut milk. Bring to a boil, reduce the heat to medium-low, cover and simmer for 5 to 8 minutes. Stir chickpeas at least once while they are simmering. Add green onions, stir and simmer chickpeas for just 1 minute more, then turn off the heat.

TO SERVE Divide curry among six plates with naan. Or, place equal portions of Grilled Coconut Kale on individual plates and gently ladle chickpea curry on top of kale—making sure that the kale is visible around the edges, as this is a very pretty combination.

WINE We serve this curry with a South American Malbec.

½ cup canola oil

1 Tbsp cumin seeds

1½ cups finely chopped onions (1 large)

12 oz tomatoes, chopped (2 medium)

1½ tsp salt

5 Tbsp finely chopped ginger

4 Tbsp finely chopped jalapeño peppers

3 cans (each 15 to 16 oz) chickpeas, drained

1 cup coconut milk, stirred

7 oz green onions, green parts only, in ¼-inch pieces (about 8 stalks)

MOONG AND MASUR
LENTIL CURRY

LENTILS

½ cup moong dal

½ cup masur dal

7½ cups water

1 Tbsp salt (if adding spinach) or 2 tsp salt

1 tsp turmeric

THIS IS A light lentil curry, which in some homes is a daily accompaniment to the evening meal. Vikram's father eats this curry as a soup before dinner at least four times a week. In our home, we make these lentils at least once a week. Although many people just boil the lentils in water, salt and turmeric and add sautéed cumin seeds at the end, we add a spicy masala, albeit a simple one, to make this curry a dish on its own with rice or chapatti. Even our daughters love this dish with plain white rice, as long as we don't add the ginger and the cayenne. Either way, it's still light enough to serve as a side to any main entrée.

Masur dal are orange, and you can buy them at most grocery stores. The tiny, yellow moong dal are available at all Indian grocers, where they are called "washed moong lentils." If you use just the orange lentils in this curry, it will be thicker. If you use just the yellow moong dal, it will be much soupier, as these lentils can almost dissolve in the water when fully cooked. For this reason, we combine both in equal amounts. It's important that you don't cover the lentils fully when they start to boil, as they will foam over the pot and create a big mess.

We like to add chopped, baby spinach leaves at the very end of the cooking process. They wilt almost immediately and the flavour and texture of the spinach blends perfectly. If you need to reheat the curry, you will most likely need to stir in another ½ to ¾ cup water.

Serves 6

LENTILS Sift through the lentils quickly to make sure there are no tiny stones or other debris. Combine moong and masur lentils in a large bowl. Wash lentils with cold water and drain; repeat 1 or 2 times.

Place lentils, water, salt and turmeric in a large pot with a tight-fitting lid and stir. On medium to high heat, bring lentils to a boil, then stir and cover most of the pot with the lid. Leave a 1-inch slit through which steam can escape; otherwise, the lentils will foam over. Reduce the heat to low and cook for another 5 to 8 minutes, or until there is very little foam left in the lentils. Cover the pan fully with the lid and cook lentils for another 30 minutes, or until tender and velvety looking.

MASALA While lentils are cooking, make the masala. In a shallow frying pan, heat ghee on medium-high heat for 45 seconds, or until completely melted. Add asafoetida and allow it to sizzle for 15 seconds, then add cumin seeds and allow them to sizzle for 15 seconds. Reduce the heat to medium. Stir in onions and sauté until brown, 8 to 10 minutes. Add ginger, tomatoes and cayenne (or jalapeño pepper) and sauté, stirring regularly, for 5 minutes or until the oil glistens on top.

Pour masala into the pot with the hot cooked lentils and stir well. (Be sure to get all of the masala from the frying pan.) While the lentils are still piping hot, stir in spinach. Just before serving, stir in cilantro.

TO SERVE Ladle piping hot curry into individual bowls and serve immediately.

WINE This lentil curry is really meant to be served as a side dish with any entrée, so drink the wine specifically paired with your chosen entrée. If you choose to serve this lentil dish with some rice or chapatti as a light main dish, we recommend a Pinot Noir Rosé.

MASALA

¼ cup ghee (page 30)

¼ tsp asafoetida

1 Tbsp cumin seeds

¾ cup finely chopped onions

1 Tbsp finely chopped ginger

¾ cup finely chopped tomatoes

½ tsp ground cayenne pepper or 1 Tbsp finely chopped jalapeño pepper

3 oz chopped baby spinach leaves (optional)

½ cup finely chopped cilantro

SEMOLINA NOODLES
WITH VEGETABLES AND LENTILS

HIS IS A full meal in itself; however, you can serve small portions as a delicious side dish in place of rice. If you serve it as a side dish, you may have to adjust the amount of jalapeño pepper, as this is a spicy dish on its own. You may want to serve it with raita (page 156) on the side.

For this recipe, we use "vermicelli" noodles from the Indian grocers. Even in India they are called vermicelli noodles on the packet. They are made from semolina and are very thin. You can buy these noodles the length of spaghetti and break them up or you can buy the smaller 1- or 2-inch-long noodles. Make sure you sauté the semolina noodles until they darken a bit; otherwise, they will stick together. If you can't find Indian-style semolina noodles, you can use the super-thin, fine egg noodles that are used in Chinese soups. Do not use regular spaghetti or other pasta noodles.

Serves 6 as a main course, 8 as a side dish

MASALA Heat oil in a medium frying pan on high heat for 1 minute. Add mustard seeds, reduce the heat to medium, stir the seeds once and wait until you hear the first popping sound. Immediately add onions and stir well to make sure the seeds don't stick and burn at the bottom of the pan. When onions are golden, in about 5 minutes, add tomatoes, salt, turmeric, coriander and jalapeño pepper. Cook the masala for 2 or 3 minutes. Add green beans and cook for 5 minutes, stirring regularly. If you prefer softer vegetables, cook green beans for another few minutes. Turn off the heat.

MASALA

½ cup canola oil

½ Tbsp black mustard seeds

2½ cups finely chopped onions (2 large)

⅓ cup chopped tomatoes (half of 1 large)

2 tsp salt

⅓ tsp turmeric

2 Tbsp ground coriander

1 Tbsp chopped jalapeño pepper

12 oz green beans, strings removed, chopped

LENTILS

¾ cup split moong dal

2 cups water

1 tsp salt

....

NOODLES

2 Tbsp canola oil

5 oz semolina
("vermicelli") noodles,
2 inches long

5 cups water

1 tsp salt

LENTILS Sift through the lentils quickly to make sure there are no tiny stones or other debris. Wash and drain split moong dal 2 or 3 times. Place lentils, water and salt in a pot and bring to a boil on medium heat. Boil gently for about 10 minutes, or until lentils are tender but not mushy.

Immediately drain lentils in a large colander to prevent them from cooking any further. Run cold water over lentils for 30 seconds, then drain for 5 minutes. Transfer to a small bowl and set aside. Rinse out the colander.

NOODLES Heat oil in a medium pot on medium heat for 2 or 3 minutes. Add noodles and sauté for 3 to 4 minutes. When the edges of the noodles are browning and the noodles look darker overall, add water and salt. Cook, stirring occasionally, for another 5 minutes, or until much of the water has evaporated and the noodles are soft. Drain noodles over a large colander and run cold water over them for 30 seconds. Gently separate the noodles with a fork, then drain completely for another 5 minutes.

FINISH CURRY Add lentils and noodles to green beans and masala. Stir gently with a fork to ensure that everything is well mixed. Just before serving, heat on low, stirring gently but regularly, for 5 minutes. If the noodles start to stick to the pot, sprinkle 2 Tbsp of water into the pan.

TO SERVE Ladle noodles into six bowls. Serve piping hot.

WINE At a private dinner, we paired this dish with the Contado Aglianico from Di Majo Norante to great compliments. If you can't find this particular wine, we recommend that you try another Aglianico wine from Italy.

Sides

CUCUMBER RAITA

2 cups plain yogurt, stirred

1 medium to large cucumber,
peeled or unpeeled

1 tsp salt

1 tsp garam masala
(page 26)

¼ tsp ground black pepper

¼ cup milk (optional)

WITH THE EXCEPTION of coconut curries, it's hard to think of any Indian dish with which we would not eat raita. This isn't to say that we eat it every time we eat Indian food, but it's refreshing with spicy dishes and is a great accompaniment to various rice pilafs. If you are serving raita with a spicy meal, you may want to leave out the garam masala in this recipe. We often eat it as a cold soup, in which case the garam masala adds a mild, satisfying zing.

Do not use bitter cucumbers or the long English cucumbers for this recipe. And, if you want to add colour to this dish, do not peel the cucumber (but be sure the peel is not bitter).

Serves 6

PLACE YOGURT in a bowl. Using a hand grater, grate cucumber and all of its water into the yogurt. Stir well to combine. Add salt, garam masala and black pepper, and mix well. If the raita appears too thick, stir in milk.

BEET AND DAIKON SALSA

 HIS "SALSA" IS a healthy, dairy-free salad that can be served with raita (page 156) or as an alternative to it, to accompany curries.

Daikon is a long white radish that is now available at most produce stores. Black salt is slightly pungent in flavour and tastes great when mixed with lemon. It is available at most Indian grocers. If you can't find the black salt, use regular salt.

Be sure to use a firm tomato, as a mushy one will ruin this recipe. It is also important to marinate the salad, as this takes away bitterness from the beet and the daikon.

Serves 6

COMBINE BEETS, daikon and tomato in a bowl. Add cilantro, black salt (or regular salt) and lemon juice and mix well. Taste and season with additional lemon and salt, if necessary. Cover with plastic wrap and refrigerate for at least 2 hours (4 hours is ideal).

13 oz beets
(2 to 3 medium),
peeled and finely diced

4 oz daikon,
peeled and finely diced

1 large, firm tomato,
finely diced

½ cup finely
chopped cilantro

1 tsp black salt
(or regular salt)

juice from ½ lemon,
or more to taste

DATE CHUTNEY

1 lb medium-size
fresh dates, pits in

2 oz tamarind pulp
(not the paste)

1 tsp cumin seeds

½ tsp ground
cayenne pepper

1 tsp salt

1 Tbsp crushed ginger

5 cups water

⅓ tsp black salt
(or regular salt)

¼ tsp garam masala
(page 26)

THIS CHUTNEY HAS a sweet, yet slightly tart (from the tamarind) and slightly pungent (from the black salt) flavour. If you don't use the black salt, you won't have this mild pungency but you will still have a delicious chutney. We actually make lots of this chutney (you can double the amounts below) and freeze it. There is no difference in taste between the thawed and the freshly made versions of this chutney.

Serve date chutney with samosas, salmon cakes (page 122), quail cakes (page 98), pakoras (page 57) or crepes. You can also chop up some apples, bananas and grapes, then stir in some chutney to make a fruit *chaat*. We sometimes stir a little chutney into yogurt and eat the date-flavoured yogurt with our meal instead of raita.

Serves 6

COMBINE ALL ingredients in a pot and bring to a boil on medium heat. Reduce the heat to medium-low and cook, uncovered, for about 30 minutes. Stir regularly. The water will evaporate quickly and the dates and tamarind will thicken. Turn off the heat and cool for 10 to 15 minutes.

Set a large fine-mesh sieve over a bowl big enough to hold 2 cups of liquid. Strain the date and tamarind mixture, in batches, through the sieve. Using a large ladle or a cooking spoon, press the paste against the sieve to extract as much as possible. Discard the date pits and the tough pulp of the tamarind. You should have a smooth chutney. Can be used right away. Will also keep in an airtight container refrigerated for up to 7 days or frozen for up to 3 months.

MINT MANGO CHUTNEY

THIS IS OUR best-selling, most popular chutney. We serve it with everything, regardless of how many spices have gone into the dish. Unlike some other chutneys, you must chill this one for at least an hour.

It's important to use mango pulp and not fresh mangoes for this chutney, as you want a smooth consistency without any chunks or strings. Our favourite is Alphonse mango pulp, which you can buy at any Indian grocer. Alphonse mangoes are specific to Mumbai and its state of Maharastra in India, and they are known to be the sweetest mangoes on Earth. Either they don't have a long harvest season or they are fragile and don't travel well—at least that's the only explanation we can come up with as to why it's so difficult and expensive to buy fresh Alphonse mangoes in New Delhi.

Years ago on a visit to Mumbai, Meeru bought two cases of Alphonse mangoes to take back to her friends and relatives in Delhi. The train journey was twelve hours long, and by the time she reached home, half of the mangoes had become overripe, mushy and too sweet. Her uncle made mango pulp from those mangoes.

Serves 6 to 8

6 oz mint leaves with stems

⅓ cup cilantro with stems

1¼ cups Alphonse mango pulp

⅓ cup coconut milk, stirred

⅛ cup white vinegar

½ Tbsp salt

1 Tbsp ground cumin

½ tsp turmeric

2 jalapeño peppers, chopped

1 Tbsp chopped garlic

WASH MINT and shake out the excess water. Remove leaves and discard stems. Wash cilantro and chop it all, including the stems.

In a food processor or blender, combine mint, cilantro (the leaves should still be wet from washing, but not dripping wet) and the remaining ingredients. If your food processor isn't large enough for all these ingredients, mix everything in a large mixing bowl first and then purée all ingredients in batches. Purée until smooth—you will still see small bits of the mint leaves.

Transfer to a bowl and cover with plastic wrap. Chill in the refrigerator for at least 1 hour. Can be used right away. Will also keep in an airtight container refrigerated for up to 7 days or frozen for up to 3 months.

CANDIED SWEET POTATO PICKLE

W E CALL THIS a "pickle" because you eat very small amounts, like other Indian pickles, with your main meal. However, there is nothing pickle-related to this recipe. We have served this sweet potato pickle as a condiment to just about any meat or seafood entrée. Four or five pieces per plate, served hot, should be enough.

This pickle will lose its flavour and texture if you overcook the sweet potato, so be sure to keep an eye on the time. You must use ghee in this recipe, as its flavour is important when combined with the sugar.

Serves 6

1½ lbs sweet potatoes, in 1½-inch or 2-inch pieces

⅓ cup demerara sugar

3 Tbsp ghee (page 30), melted

½ tsp turmeric

½ Tbsp salt

½ tsp ground cayenne pepper

PREHEAT THE OVEN to 450°F. In a mixing bowl, combine sweet potatoes, sugar, ghee, turmeric, salt and cayenne. Stir well and make sure potatoes are well covered in the spice mixture. Pour potatoes onto a baking tray, cover with aluminum foil and bake for 20 minutes.

Carefully remove the tray from the oven and remove the foil. Lightly stir potatoes to distribute ghee and sugar evenly. Poke sweet potato with a knife to see if it is cooked. If sweet potato is still slightly raw in the middle, replace aluminum foil and bake for another 5 minutes. Be very careful not to overcook sweet potatoes.

Remove sweet potatoes from the oven. Uncover immediately and stir carefully.

GRILLED COCONUT KALE

1 lb kale with stems

3 cups coconut milk

1 Tbsp salt

1 tsp ground
cayenne pepper

1 tsp paprika

¼ cup lemon juice

HIS SIMPLE VEGETABLE dish is always on our seasonal menus in one way or another. You can't eat very much, but it's a great side dish that also makes a great garnish. The weight of the kale given below is with the stalks, as you buy it from the market. It's important, though, to discard the stalks.

The grilled kale should be eaten warm. Depending on what you are serving it with, make sure your entrée is ready to serve at the same time as the kale.

Serves 6

WASH KALE thoroughly and cut off the stalks. (The tough stalks take too long to grill and are difficult to chew.) Cut kale leaves about 6 inches long. Keep the smaller leaves as well.

In a pot, melt coconut milk on low heat until thoroughly mixed and just lukewarm. Transfer to a large stainless steel bowl and add salt, cayenne, paprika and lemon juice. Stir in kale leaves, cover with plastic wrap and refrigerate for at least 4 hours.

Preheat a barbeque or stovetop cast-iron grill to high heat. Remove kale from the refrigerator and stir well to make sure leaves are well covered in the marinade. Using metal tongs, place kale leaves in a single layer on the grill. Cook one side for 30 seconds (smaller leaves) to 45 seconds (larger leaves). Turn leaves over and grill for another 30 to 45 seconds, or until they have visibly softened. Serve immediately.

CABBAGE IN MILD YOGURT

AND MUSTARD SEED CURRY

I N NORTH AMERICA, cabbage is associated with coleslaw and lunch. In India, cabbage is one of the most popular vegetables and is used in a variety of vegetarian dishes. At Vij's, we serve this curried cabbage as a side to any of our meat dishes.

The size of the cabbage pieces doesn't matter—if you prefer chunkier pieces, then cut them that way—but be careful not to overcook them, as the cabbage will become sweet and lose its crunch. We recommend that you use 4% milkfat yogurt, and nothing less. Actually, if you aren't watching your weight, it's best to use 10% milkfat Mediterranean-style yogurt. If you are lactose intolerant, substitute 1½ cups stirred coconut milk for the yogurt.

Serves 6

PLACE CABBAGE pieces in a colander and rinse well. Drain cabbage of any excess water.

Heat oil in a large frying pan on medium-high for 1 minute. Add asafoetida and allow it to sizzle for 10 seconds. Add mustard seeds and cook until you hear the first popping sound, about 1 minute. Immediately turn off the heat. (The popping sound means that the seeds have cooked and are beginning to burn.)

After 5 minutes, stir in yogurt and turn on the heat to medium, stirring continuously for 1 minute. Add salt, cumin, turmeric and coriander. Cook for about 5 minutes, or until the oil glistens. Add cabbage and stir well. Make sure the masala and cabbage are completely combined.

If you are ready to serve the cabbage, reduce the heat to low and continue cooking it for 5 minutes. Otherwise turn off the heat and reheat on medium-high for 3 to 4 minutes just before serving. Can be used right away. Will keep refrigerated for up to 1 day in a sealed container, but this dish loses its texture after a day in the fridge.

1 head green cabbage, in 1 inch × 1 inch × 3 inch pieces

½ cup canola oil

1 tsp asafoetida

1 Tbsp + 1 tsp black mustard seeds

1 ½ cups plain yogurt, stirred

1 Tbsp salt

1 Tbsp ground cumin

1 tsp turmeric

1 Tbsp ground coriander

CASSAVA FRIES

4 lbs frozen cassava

10 cups water

1 Tbsp salt

6 cups oil for deep-frying

½ tsp salt or ½ tsp black salt

½ tsp ground
cayenne pepper

ASSAVA, WHICH IS also known as mogo or yucca, originally comes from Central and South America and is eaten
throughout the region as a staple food. This vegetable is also
eaten throughout West Africa. Although cassava is often mashed before
being eaten, we boil then fry it to make fries that are not as rich and
starchy as the ones made from potatoes. Our cassava fries are crisp, yet
light and flaky on the inside.

We find that frozen whole cassava works just as well as fresh cassava,
and means less work. And since there are so many ways to eat these fries,
we often make this recipe in large portions. We serve them as a side
dish with just about any meat entrée, and we also serve them as a finger
food to customers waiting in our lounge for a table. While we prefer the
slightly tart and pungent flavour of black salt to sprinkle lightly on the hot
fries, you can just as easily use regular salt. If you wish to serve the fries
as a small side dish, halve this recipe.

Serves 8 to 10

COMBINE FROZEN cassava, water and 1 Tbsp salt in large pot. Bring to
boil on high heat, then reduce the heat to medium, cover and boil for
25 minutes, or until tender. Drain cassava and cool for 15 minutes.

Cut cassava in half. With a paring knife, remove the tough, stringlike
fibre that runs the length of the cassava. Discard the fibre, then cut the
cassava in pieces 3 to 4 inches long about ½ inch wide and ½ inch thick,
similar to the size of french fries.

Line a baking tray with paper towels. Preheat a deep fryer to high heat
or heat oil in a large heavy-bottomed pan on high heat for 5 minutes.
Drop a small piece of cassava into the oil. It should immediately float to
the top and sizzle. Once the oil is hot enough, place fries in the pan and
fry for 3 to 4 minutes, or until golden. Using a slotted spoon, transfer fries
to the paper towels to drain any excess oil. Sprinkle fries with the ½ tsp of
salt (or black salt) and the cayenne while they are still hot.

CAULIFLOWER AND POTATO PURÉE

AS A SUBSTITUTE for rice and naan, we serve this purée with many of our meats, mostly our grilled or seared meats. This purée tastes great with Panfried Tomato and Coriander Quail Cakes (page 98), Demerara Sugar and Tamarind–marinated Beef Tenderloin (page 73) or Yogurt- and Tamarind-marinated Grilled Chicken (page 93).

Serves 6

PREHEAT THE OVEN to 450°F. In a large roasting pan, combine cauliflower, potatoes, garam masala, salt and cayenne. Stir well and make sure cauliflower and potatoes are well covered in the spice mixture. Cover the pan with a tight-fitting lid or with aluminum foil. Bake for 30 minutes, or until cauliflower and potatoes are completely soft and almost mushy. Cool completely for 1 hour.

Transfer cauliflower, potatoes and spices to a food processor. (Make sure you get all the spices and don't leave them in the roasting pan.) Add cream in small batches and purée until smooth. Transfer to a serving dish and stir in cilantro.

1½ lbs cauliflower, washed, drained of excess water and cut in about 10 large chunks

12 oz potato (1 large), peeled and cut in 2-inch cubes

1 Tbsp garam masala (page 26)

1 Tbsp salt

½ tsp ground cayenne pepper

½ cup whipping cream

½ cup chopped cilantro

TURMERIC NEW POTATOES

2 lbs new potatoes

¼ cup canola oil

1½ cups chopped
onions (1 large)

1 tsp turmeric

1 Tbsp salt

½ tsp ground
cayenne pepper

¼ cup water

5 oz baby spinach
(optional)

WE SERVE THIS dish at Vij's with our meat entrées as an alternative to rice. If you can't cut the potatoes as thin as the recipe calls for, just add a little extra water to ensure that the potatoes get fully cooked without sticking to the pan. We like to add pre-washed baby spinach at the very end, but this is optional. Grocery stores usually sell 5-ounce bags of baby spinach.

Serves 6 to 8

WASH AND SCRUB the potatoes but do not peel them. Cut each potato in ¼-inch (or slightly thinner) rounds.

Heat oil in a heavy frying pan on medium heat for 1 minute. Add onions and sauté for 5 minutes, or until golden. Add turmeric, salt and cayenne, stir well and cook for 1 minute. Add potatoes and water and bring to a light boil. Gently stir the potatoes. Reduce the heat to low, cover and cook for about 10 minutes. If the potatoes are sticking or burning, add another ¼ cup water. Gently stir the potatoes again. Cover and cook for another 5 minutes, or until potatoes are cooked. These potatoes should maintain their shape and not get too soft. If using spinach, gently stir it in 1 minute before turning off the heat.

Serve warm from the frying pan. If you need to reheat the potatoes, transfer them to a nonstick frying pan and heat them on low.

CUMIN BASMATI RICE

O NCE YOU KNOW the water-to-rice ratios for cooking basmati rice, you can play around with various additions, which can turn plain rice into an entire meal if you wish. We always soak basmati rice in cold water for 10 to 15 minutes before cooking. This ensures that the rice is soft and fluffy. You don't need to drain the rice in a colander or a sieve, just pour off as much water as possible. You don't even need to add the cumin in this recipe—we've included it for added flavour, but many Indian homes serve plain, salted basmati rice.

Some brands of basmati rice are now cultivated in the United States. The real white basmati rice, however, comes from a specific region in northern India, in the Himalayan foothills. It has been growing there for thousands of years, and unless you have difficulty securing Indian basmati rice, we don't see any reason for purchasing any other type. Nothing can beat the flavour, aroma or texture of Himalayan-grown basmati rice.

Serves 6

2 cups basmati rice

3 cups cold water for soaking

¼ cup canola oil

1 Tbsp cumin seeds

1 cup finely chopped onions (1 medium-large)

3¾ cups water for cooking

WASH BASMATI rice twice in cold water. Soak rice in the 3 cups of cold water for 15 minutes, or while you are sautéing the cumin seeds and onions.

Heat oil in a medium pot for 1 minute on medium-high heat. Add cumin seeds, stir and allow to sizzle for about 30 seconds. Add onions and sauté for 4 to 5 minutes, until just the edges are brown (for a sweeter onion flavour), or for 3 to 4 minutes more, until brown (for a stronger flavour). Turn off the heat.

Drain the rice as much as possible. Add rice and the 3¾ cups of water to onions, and stir well to combine. Turn on the heat to high and bring to a boil. Once the water is boiling vigorously, lower the heat to just a simmer, cover the pot and cook for 18 to 20 minutes. Turn off the heat and allow the rice to sit, covered, for 5 minutes. Take off the lid, fluff the rice with a fork and serve.

CAULIFLOWER RICE PILAF

RICE

2 cups basmati rice

3 cups water for soaking

3¾ cups water for boiling

½ Tbsp butter

¾ tsp salt

CAULIFLOWER

2 tsp cumin seeds

2 to 3 Tbsp canola oil

1 large onion, chopped

10 cloves

1¼ tsp turmeric

1 jalapeño pepper, chopped (optional)

1½ tsp salt

1 cauliflower, in 1-inch florets

½ cup chopped cilantro, with stems

 HIS CAULIFLOWER RICE pilaf tastes great with raita (page 156) or plain yogurt as a light meal on its own. Otherwise, it's a great accompaniment to any meat curry. When cutting the cauliflower, use as much of its stalks as possible. Unless it's super-large, the relative size of the cauliflower doesn't matter. If it is super-large, don't use all of it.

Serves 6

RICE Wash basmati rice twice in cold water. Soak rice in the 3 cups of water for 15 to 20 minutes. Drain rice.

In a medium pot with a lid, combine rice, the 3¾ cups of water, butter and salt on high heat. As soon as the rice starts to boil vigorously, reduce the heat to low, cover and simmer for 18 to 20 minutes.

Turn off the heat, but do not remove the lid. Allow rice to sit for 5 minutes, then remove the lid and set aside.

CAULIFLOWER In a separate frying pan or a wok, heat cumin seeds in oil on medium to high heat. Once seeds have sizzled for 30 to 45 seconds, reduce the heat to medium and add onions and cloves. Sauté onions for 8 to 10 minutes, or until brown. Add turmeric, jalapeño pepper and salt, and sauté for another 2 minutes. Add cauliflower, stir well and stir-fry for 5 minutes. Reduce the heat to medium-low, cover and cook for another 5 to 8 minutes, until cauliflower is cooked but still firm and not too soft.

Add cauliflower to rice and combine well. Add cilantro and stir with a large fork until the rice is completely yellow from the turmeric.

BROWN BASMATI RICE
AND FRENCH GREEN LENTIL PILAF

W E PREFER TO use French green lentils in our rice pilafs, as they are firm and keep their shape instead of getting mashed into the rice. When we make lentil curry to go on the side with rice, we use either moong or masur lentils, which soak in the spices of the curry and become soft and velvety.

Brown basmati rice doesn't taste anything like regular basmati rice since it's brown and has that distinct nutty flavour, but it is a longer and flakier grain than regular long-grain brown rice. You can use regular long-grain brown rice instead.

We serve this pilaf with Long Green Beans and New Potatoes in Mustard Seed Curry (page 140). You can, however, serve it with any curry that is dairy free—as yogurt or cream doesn't complement the coconut milk in this pilaf.

Serves 6

1 cup French green lentils

1 cup brown basmati rice

½ cup canola oil

½ tsp asafoetida

1 Tbsp cumin seeds

1 cup finely chopped onions (1 medium-large)

1½-inch stick of cinnamon

½ tsp turmeric

1 Tbsp salt

½ tsp ground cayenne pepper

7 cups water

1 cup coconut milk, stirred

COMBINE LENTILS and rice in a small bowl. Wash them twice in cold water and drain them well. Set aside.

In a medium pot with a tight-fitting lid, heat oil on high heat for 1 minute. Add asafoetida and allow it to sizzle for 15 seconds. Add cumin seeds, stir immediately and cook until they sizzle for 30 seconds. Reduce the heat to medium, add onions and cinnamon stick and stir them well into the cumin. Sauté onions for 8 to 10 minutes, or until brown. Add turmeric, salt and cayenne. Cook for about 1 minute.

Add water, coconut milk and the mixed lentils and brown rice. Increase the heat to high and bring to a boil. As soon as water is boiling vigorously, reduce the heat to low, stir once more and cover. Simmer rice and lentils for at least 1 hour, then lift the lid, stir pilaf and check to see if the rice is cooked. It takes about 1 hour 10 minutes on average. When done, turn off the heat, and replace the lid. Allow rice to sit for 5 minutes, then remove the lid and set aside.

GINGER, JALAPEÑO
AND COCONUT BROWN RICE PILAF

BROWN RICE

1½ cups long-grain
brown rice

5 cups water

1 Tbsp salt

1 Tbsp canola oil

**GINGER-JALAPEÑO-COCONUT
MASALA**

½ cup canola oil

1½ cups finely chopped
onions (1 large)

3 Tbsp finely chopped garlic

3 Tbsp finely chopped
ginger (1¼ oz)

1 large jalapeño pepper,
finely chopped

1½ cups coconut milk,
stirred

HIS PILAF LOOKS and tastes a lot like a creamy risotto. We cook the rice and the ginger-jalapeño-coconut masala separately and then mix them together. It's best to follow the instructions on the bag of the brown rice you purchase, but we have also given the instructions below. The rice should be cooked thoroughly.

At Vij's we serve this pilaf with the Duck Breast in Lime Leaf Curry (page 101), but you could serve this with many of the meat dishes in this book that aren't heavy on the cream or yogurt.

Serves 6

BROWN RICE Wash rice in cold water. Drain well. Combine rice, water, salt and oil in a medium pot with a tight-fitting lid. On high heat, bring to a boil. Immediately reduce the heat to low, cover and cook for 50 minutes. Check to see if rice is cooked. If it is not, continue cooking on low heat, covered, for another 10 minutes. Turn off the heat, but do not remove the lid. Allow rice to sit for 5 minutes, then remove the lid and set aside.

GINGER-JALAPEÑO-COCONUT MASALA Heat oil in a medium frying pan on medium-high heat for 1 minute. Add onions and sauté until slightly dark brown, about 8 minutes. They should look a little burned around the edges. Add garlic and sauté for another 2 minutes, stirring regularly. (Stirring regularly keeps the onions from burning while the garlic is cooking.) Add ginger and jalapeño pepper, stir and cook for 1 more minute. Add coconut milk, stir well and bring to a boil. Reduce the heat to low and cook for 5 to 8 minutes. You should see some oil glistening on top of the curry.

Pour masala into rice. Stir well and serve.

PEARL BARLEY PILAF

SOMETIMES IT'S NICE to eat something other than rice and bread with Indian food. This barley pilaf can be served in place of a rice pilaf with any dish and many people actually prefer it, as the barley can take more spices than rice. Unlike rice pilafs, though, we don't think pearl barley tastes good with raita or yogurt.

Serves 6

PEARL BARLEY Rinse barley in cold water. Combine water, oil and salt in a medium pot and heat on high heat. When water reaches a vigorous boil, add barley. Reduce the heat to low, cover and simmer for 25 minutes. Stir barley, replace lid and turn off the heat. Allow to sit for 5 to 10 minutes.

MASALA In a separate frying pan, heat oil on medium-high for 1 minute. Add onions and sauté for 5 to 8 minutes, or until golden. Add garlic and sauté for another 3 to 4 minutes. Add ginger and jalapeño pepper, then stir and cook for 2 to 3 minutes. Add barley to the masala, add cilantro and stir well.

If reheating the next day, add ½ cup water to the barley pilaf and heat it on medium heat. As soon as you see steam, reduce the heat to low, cover and simmer for 5 minutes. Serve immediately.

PEARL BARLEY

¾ cup pearl barley

3 cups water

½ Tbsp canola oil

½ Tbsp salt

MASALA

¼ cup canola oil

1½ cups chopped onions (1 large)

2 Tbsp finely chopped garlic

1½ Tbsp finely chopped ginger

1 Tbsp finely chopped jalapeño pepper

⅓ cup chopped cilantro

CHAPATTI DOUGH

CHAPATTI FLOUR IS a mixture of mostly whole-wheat, bran and/or all-purpose flour. Chapatti, known as roti in Punjabi, is the staple bread for Indians. Growing up, we were required to eat at least two chapattis with our dinner, and a day without roti was considered an unhealthy day. All Indian stores carry chapatti flour, and we use the variety that contains a higher percentage of whole-wheat and bran flours than all-purpose flour.

Looking at the length of this recipe, you may get the impression that making chapattis is a complicated process. It's actually very simple. You will have to make this recipe a couple of times before you get the hang of it, but if you like chapattis, it's worth it. We have yet to find store-bought chapattis that taste as delicious as these coming hot off the stove.

A *thava* is either a flat or slightly concave iron pan specifically designed for making chapattis. Some thavas are thicker than others, but the thin, heavy ones are the best. Although they take a little longer to heat up, they retain the heat better and your chapattis won't burn as quickly as they would on lighter-weight thavas. Although you can buy a thava from most Indian grocers, we don't recommend that you go out and buy one right away, unless you know you will make chapattis more than once. Instead, use a heavy-bottomed nonstick or regular frying pan or a flat iron pan. Your chapattis may not fluff up as they would on a thava, and they may be slightly crispier, but they will taste good and you will know whether or not you will make them again!

It is crucial that you make the chapattis right next to where you will be cooking them, because you must roll them out and cook them one at a time. Rolled-out chapatti dough becomes very soft while sitting at room temperature and can easily fall apart during the cooking process, so you don't want to be transporting the chapattis too far or allowing them to sit too long. Make sure that you have a small cotton tea towel on hand with which to fluff the chapattis.

It is difficult to give a precise chapatti flour to water ratio, so don't hesitate to use a few tablespoons more or less water than we have written—the key is to attain a smooth dough.

Chapattis are best eaten within a few minutes of cooking. Many people like to spread them with a bit of butter or ghee. If you are serving them at the table, do so within an hour of cooking. We serve them mostly with vegetarian dishes.

PLACE CHAPATTI flour in a large mixing bowl. Slowly add water and keep mixing the water into the flour with your hands. Knead flour and water until you have a ball of smooth dough without any clumps of flour in it. The more you knead the dough, the better your chapatti will turn out. The less sticky the dough, the better it will be for making chapattis. If the dough is too sticky, rub the 1 tsp of oil on your hands and continue kneading until the dough is no longer sticky. Be careful not to use too much oil, as chapattis are meant to be light and airy. Form the dough in an egg shape, cover it with plastic wrap and allow it to rest in the refrigerator for at least 1 hour. This will make the dough easier to roll.

When you are ready to start rolling out your chapattis, heat the thava on medium-high heat (if you are using a frying pan, heat it on medium heat) for 5 to 7 minutes.

Line a plate with a large cotton napkin. This is where you will place the cooked chapattis to keep them warm.

Spread the ½ cup of flour for rolling on another large plate. Unwrap the chilled dough and divide it in six equal portions. Dab one portion in a little flour. Using your hands, roll the dough into a smooth ball. Once you have a smooth ball, roll it in the flour, covering it completely but lightly. With a rolling pin, roll out the ball until it is 3 to 4 inches in diameter. When the chapatti starts sticking to your rolling pin, cover both sides of the chapatti once again in the flour, completely but lightly. Roll out the chapatti until it is 8 inches in diameter.

Carefully lift the chapatti and place it in the palm of one hand, spreading out your fingers to support it. Gently flip the chapatti onto the hot thava (or frying pan). The chapatti should be flat, without any folds. Cook chapatti on one side for 40 to 50 seconds, or until it looks slightly darker and little bubbles start to form. Using tongs (or your fingers, if you have enough experience), turn over the chapatti. Cook for another 40 to 50 seconds, or until the bubbles increase in size. Flip chapatti over again. You'll notice that the bubbles are now slightly browned and are quickly forming. (If the bubbles haven't changed colour at all, then slightly increase the heat. If the chapatti is sticking to the thava, then slightly decrease the heat.)

1 cup chapatti flour

about ⅔ cup water

1 tsp canola oil (optional)

½ cup chapatti flour for rolling

½ tsp canola oil for rolling (optional)

1 Tbsp ghee (page 30) or butter for spreading on cooked chapattis (optional)

To fluff the chapatti, bunch a small cotton tea towel in one hand and gently press down and out to the edges of the chapatti until the bubbles expand. Be careful not to press too hard on the bubbles or they can pop, releasing hot air that can burn your hand. Do this for up to 1 minute. You should be moving the chapatti around on the thava (or frying pan) as you are doing this. Turn over the chapatti one last time and gently press on the bubbles as they expand further, up to 1 minute more. Transfer the cooked chapatti to the cloth-lined plate.

A chapatti can have many bubbles or only a few. If your entire chapatti is one big bubble, then you have made the perfect chapatti! Repeat this procedure with the remaining five portions of dough, until you have six cooked chapattis. Stack the cooked chapattis on the napkin, wrapping the material completely around them. This will keep them warm and soft.

Rub warm chapattis with ½ tsp of ghee or butter. Serve immediately.

SPLIT CHICKPEA LENTIL CHAPATTIS

I N INDIA, THE vegetarian leftovers from last night's dinner are often mashed up and kneaded into the chapatti dough. The chapattis are then eaten with pickles and/or yogurt for brunch or lunch. They pack well in tiffin carriers (Indian canister-style lunch boxes) and are relatively quick and easy to eat.

Before you make this recipe, we strongly recommend that you first make the basic chapattis (page 172). We make a lentil curry and knead it into the chapatti dough as a combination side vegetable/bread with a meat dish. The split chickpea lentils, also known as *channa dal,* mix well into the dough, making the chapattis much easier to roll than if they were made with vegetables or harder-textured lentils. These lentils will take about 1½ to 2 hours to boil, plus an hour or two to cool. You can make them the day before you make the chapattis. You will have some leftover lentil curry from this recipe.

This recipe makes a lot of chapattis, but it is too time consuming to make only six or eight chapattis, unless you really do have just a little bit of leftover curry. Unlike regular chapattis, these lentil chapattis keep well and taste just as good when they are reheated. Wrap uneaten lentil chapattis in aluminum foil, being sure to cover them completely. Reheat them either in a toaster oven on the "toast" setting or on a preheated thava.

There are many ways to serve these chapattis. Spread a little ghee or butter on each warm chapatti and serve them with any seafood, poultry or meat curry. Or for a casual meal, make the kebobs on page 64 or 66 and roll them in these chapattis before eating. Spread a little plain yogurt or chutney on the rolled kebobs.

Makes 20 chapattis

LENTIL CURRY

1 cup split chickpea
lentils (channa dal)

11 cups water

1½ Tbsp salt

½ Tbsp ground
cayenne pepper

½ Tbsp turmeric

⅓ cup ghee (page 30)

½ cup finely chopped
onions (1 small)

2 Tbsp finely chopped
jalapeño peppers

1 cup chopped cilantro

....

CHAPATTIS

1½ cups chapatti flour

2 cups lentil curry, cold

1 to 3 tsp canola oil
(optional, for
kneading and rolling)

¾ cup chapatti
flour for rolling

¼ cup ghee (page 30) or
canola oil for the thava

LENTIL CURRY Combine lentils, water, salt, cayenne and turmeric in a large pot on high heat. Bring to a boil. The lentils will foam up as soon as they start to boil, so immediately reduce the heat to low to prevent the foam from spilling over the side of the pot. Partially cover lentils with a lid and boil gently. As soon as the foam reduces, cover the pot completely and simmer lentils for about 2 hours, stirring every 20 minutes. When the lentils are completely soft and velvety, turn off the heat.

Melt ghee in a small frying pan on medium heat and sauté onions for about 10 minutes, or until nicely browned but not burned. Add jalapeño peppers and sauté for another minute or so. When lentils are fully cooked, stir in the onion-jalapeño mixture and cilantro. Remove from the heat and cool completely for at least 1 hour. Refrigerate curry, covered, for at least 1 hour, or until you are ready to make the chapattis. Will keep refrigerated in a covered container for up to 3 days.

CHAPATTIS Combine chapatti flour and lentil curry in a large mixing bowl. Mix well and knead until you have a ball of smooth dough without any clumps of flour in it. In the beginning this will be very sticky, but continue to mix and knead. If the dough continues to be too sticky, rub 1 to 2 tsp oil on your hands and continue kneading until the dough is no longer sticky. The dough is then ready to use. (If you are not ready to start cooking the chapattis, cover the dough with plastic wrap and refrigerate it for up to 1 day.)

When you are ready to start rolling out your chapattis, heat the thava on medium-high heat (if you are using a frying pan, heat it on medium heat) for 5 to 7 minutes.

Line a plate with a large cotton napkin. This is where you will place the cooked chapattis to keep them warm.

Spread the ¾ cup of flour for rolling on another large plate. Unwrap the chilled dough and pull off enough to make a ball 2½ inches in diameter. Dab the dough in a little flour. Using your hands, roll this dough into a smooth ball. If the dough sticks to your hands, rub ½ tsp oil on them. Once you have a smooth ball, roll it in the flour, covering it completely but lightly. With a rolling pin, roll out the ball until it is 3 to 4 inches in diameter. When the chapatti starts sticking to your rolling pin, cover both sides of the chapatti once again in the flour, completely but lightly. Roll out the chapatti until it is 8 inches in diameter.

Spread ½ tsp of the ghee (or canola oil) on the heated thava (or frying pan). Carefully lift the chapatti and place it in the palm of one hand, spreading out your fingers to support it. Gently flip the chapatti onto the hot thava (or frying pan). The chapatti should be flat, without any folds. Cook chapatti on one side for 40 to 50 seconds, or until it looks slightly darker and little bubbles start to form. Using a large spatula or tongs (or your fingers, if you have enough experience), turn over the chapatti. Cook for another 40 to 50 seconds, or until the bubbles increase in size. Flip chapatti over again. You'll notice that the bubbles are now browned. (If the bubbles haven't changed colour at all, then slightly increase the heat. If the chapatti is sticking to the thava, then slightly decrease the heat.)

To fluff the chapatti, bunch a small cotton tea towel in one hand and gently press down and out to the edges of the chapatti until the bubbles expand. Be careful not to press too hard on the bubbles or they can pop, releasing hot air that can burn your hand. Do this for up to 1 minute. You should be moving the chapatti around on the thava (or frying pan) as you are doing this. Turn over the chapatti one last time and gently press on the bubbles as they expand further, up to 1 minute more. Transfer the cooked chapatti to the cloth-lined plate.

A chapatti can have many bubbles or only a few, and lentil chapattis generally don't fluff up as much as regular chapattis because the lentils make them heavier. Repeat this procedure with the remaining dough, until you have used it all. For each new chapatti, spread ½ tsp ghee or oil on the thava (or frying pan). Stack the cooked chapattis on the napkin, wrapping the material completely around them. This will keep them warm and soft.

Will keep in the refrigerator for up to 3 days well wrapped in aluminum foil.

CAULIFLOWER, HONEY
AND GARLIC PARANTAS

FILLING

1 small head cauliflower,
very finely chopped

1 Tbsp salt

½ Tbsp mango powder

1 Tbsp ground coriander

½ cup chopped cilantro

⅓ cup canola oil
or ghee (page 30)

12 to 13 cloves garlic,
thinly sliced

1 cup honey

A PARANTA IS A stuffed chapatti. Although this is considered a relatively easy recipe for seasoned Indian cooks (albeit time consuming), grasping the technique of making a paranta can be difficult at first. Before you make this recipe, we strongly recommend that you first make the basic chapattis (page 172). You may want to have one person roll out a paranta while another person cooks one. The timing can be tricky since you want to cook the paranta as soon as it has been rolled. Once you get the hang of it, this is a perfect recipe for a leisurely brunch. We have fond memories of sitting at the table for hours being served hot parantas.

You can serve the parantas with some raita (page 156) or on their own, or make smaller ones and serve them with dinner. Parantas can be stuffed with anything you choose, as long as it isn't runny. At a minimum you can stuff them with salted mashed potatoes, which is how our daughters enjoy them.

When chopping the cauliflower, you can grate it in a food processor, but make sure that you don't grate it too finely as this alters the flavour (it tastes like mushy cauliflower once it's heated) and texture of the cauliflower. When you eat the paranta, you want to be able to bite into very, very small pieces of cauliflower rather than a puréed cauliflower. Just remember that you have to roll out the dough that is stuffed with the cauliflower. Big pieces of cauliflower will tear through the dough. You will also need a thava, or a stovetop cast-iron pan.

Serves 6

FILLING In a large mixing bowl, thoroughly combine cauliflower with salt, mango powder, coriander and cilantro. Set aside.

Heat oil (or ghee) in a small, heavy-bottomed frying pan on medium heat. Add garlic and sauté until golden brown. Stir in honey, then reduce the heat to low. Stir for 3 to 4 minutes, or until honey melts and mixes with the garlic. Remove from the heat and cool until it is warm.

While it is still warm (but not hot), pour the honey-garlic mixture into the cauliflower and stir well. Set aside.

3 cups chapatti flour

2 cups less 2 Tbsp water

1 to 3 tsp canola oil
(optional, for kneading
and rolling)

1 cup chapatti flour
for rolling

½ to ¾ cup ghee (page 30),
canola oil or butter

PARANTAS Place chapatti flour in a large mixing bowl. Slowly add water and keep mixing the water into the flour with your hands. Knead flour and water until you have a ball of smooth dough without any clumps of flour in it. If the dough is too sticky, rub ½ tsp oil on your hands and continue kneading until the dough is no longer sticky. Form the dough in an egg shape, cover it with plastic wrap and allow it to rest in the refrigerator for at least 1 hour. This will make the dough easier to roll.

It is crucial that you roll out and cook the parantas one at a time. Rolled-out paranta dough becomes very soft while sitting at room temperature and can easily fall apart during the cooking process, so you don't want to be transporting the parantas too far or allowing them to sit too long. Make sure that you have a small cotton tea towel on hand with which to help flip the parantas.

Line a plate with aluminum foil. This is where you will place the cooked parantas to keep them warm.

When you are ready to start rolling out your parantas, heat the thava on medium-high heat (if you are using a frying pan, heat it on medium heat) for 5 to 7 minutes.

Spread the 1 cup of flour for rolling on another large plate. Unwrap the chilled dough and divide it in twelve equal portions. Dab one portion in a little flour. Using your hands, roll the dough into a smooth ball. If the dough sticks to your hands, rub ½ tsp oil on them. Once you have a smooth ball, roll it in the flour, covering it completely but lightly. With a rolling pin, roll out the ball until it is 4 to 5 inches in diameter.

Place 3 Tbsp of the cauliflower mixture in the middle of the rolled-out paranta. Bring all the edges in to the centre so cauliflower is enclosed inside the chapatti dough and you now have a stuffed ball of chapatti dough. Carefully roll this ball in the flour, covering it completely but lightly. With a rolling pin, roll out this ball until it is 5 to 6 inches in diameter, or until it starts to stick to the rolling pin. Dip both sides of the paranta in flour again and continue rolling until the paranta is 8 inches in diameter. (The first paranta is your practice paranta, so stop when the rolling is no longer easy. Don't worry if it is bigger or smaller than 8 inches.) Practice is what makes this recipe easier and easier. The more comfortable you get with the rolling, the more cauliflower you will be able to fit in the paranta.

Spread ½ to 1 tsp of ghee or oil on the heated thava (or frying pan). Carefully place the paranta onto the hot thava (or frying pan). As the edges cook through, in 3 to 4 minutes, bunch up a tea towel in one hand, then using this hand and a spatula, turn sizzling paranta over and cook for another 3 to 4 minutes. Turn paranta over again and spread ½ to 1 tsp more of ghee or oil on the paranta. Cook until both sides are slightly crispy and golden brown with darker brown patches throughout. Transfer the cooked paranta to the foil-lined plate. (This process is like cooking a more complicated grilled-cheese sandwich.)

Repeat this procedure with the remaining eleven portions of dough, until you have twelve cooked parantas. For each new paranta, spread ½ tsp ghee (or oil or butter) on the thava (or frying pan). Eat parantas hot off the grill or stack them on the foil, if you will not be eating them right away.

Uneaten parantas will keep, wrapped in foil, in the refrigerator for up to 2 days. Reheat them, still wrapped in foil, in a preheated 375°F oven for 10 to 12 minutes. If you reheat all 12, it will take 20 minutes. They will not be crispy but they will still be warm and delicious.

Desserts & Drinks

RICOTTA AND ALMOND PUDDING

½ cup ghee (page 30)

½ cup green lentil flour

about ¾ cup tightly packed
raw sugar or 1 cup
demerara sugar

1 cup water

½ cup ricotta cheese

⅛ to ¼ cup raw, unsalted,
chopped almonds
(optional)

THIS RICH DESSERT, called halwa, is quick to make and tastes great with an after-dinner cup of coffee or tea. The green lentil flour is referred to as "moong flour." You can buy it and the raw sugar at any Indian grocer. You can also use demerara sugar instead of the raw sugar. We prefer not to use regular white sugar, as we feel that it leaves this dessert tasting flat.

Although we don't usually recommend any microwaving, the best way to reheat this pudding is in the microwave, in a glass bowl. You may wish to heat it for 30 seconds on high, stir and heat for another 30 seconds. You shouldn't have to reheat this pudding for any more than 1 minute. Serve with a hot cup of coffee or tea.

Makes 6 servings (⅓ cup each)

MELT GHEE in a pot on medium-low heat. Stir in flour and cook for 8 minutes, stirring regularly. The flour will darken to a brownish-orange as it cooks. Reduce the heat to low and add sugar. Stir in water. If using raw sugar, dissolve it by gently mashing the chunks with a spoon. When sugar has completely dissolved, add ricotta. Cook, stirring, on low heat for 5 to 8 minutes. Add chopped almonds.

TO SERVE Stir pudding well, then spoon into six small bowls. Serve hot or warm.

MANGO KULFI

IN INDIA, KULFI, or Indian ice cream, is one of the most popular desserts. Street vendors sell it as popsicles, and five-star restaurants serve it as a fancy dessert. We once took the kulfi off our menu, and an Indian family was shocked and disappointed beyond belief.

Once you have a good recipe for making kulfi, you can add almost any flavour. We add a bit of white rice flour to give the kulfi a slightly softer texture, and we find the rice flour also soaks in whatever flavour you choose to add. Since mango pulp is presweetened, remember that you may have to add more sugar if you choose another flavour of kulfi.

If you know that you'll be making kulfi quite often, visit an Indian grocer and buy individual kulfi containers. They are cone-shaped tins with screw-on lids and they come in different sizes. Kulfi will keep frozen for up to 1 month in kulfi containers or up to 3 days in small ceramic bowls sealed tightly with plastic wrap. Kulfi is usually eaten frozen like ice cream. If you prefer, serve it warmed, which is how Meeru likes it.

Makes 8 servings (½ cup each)

1 cup whipping cream

6 cups whole milk

1 Tbsp white rice flour

4 Tbsp sugar

¾ cup Alphonse mango pulp

⅓ cup chopped pistachios (optional)

IN A HEAVY POT, combine cream, milk and rice flour with a whisk until smooth. Bring to a slow boil on medium-low heat, stirring regularly. Once the mixture starts to boil, reduce the heat to low. Cook for 45 minutes, stirring regularly and scraping the milk that sticks to the side of the pot back into the mixture. As it cooks, the mixture will begin to thicken. When it is cream-coloured and has the consistency of whipping cream, turn off the heat and stir in sugar. Set aside to cool for 15 minutes. Stir in mango pulp (and pistachios, if desired).

At Vij's, we pour the kulfi into small brightly coloured ceramic bowls, cover them tightly with plastic wrap, then place the bowls in the freezer. Pour ½ cup of the mango-kulfi mixture into each of 8 ceramic bowls or ramekins. Cover each bowl or ramekin with plastic wrap and freeze for at least 6 hours or up to 24 hours. (Regular-size kulfi containers also take about ½ cup.)

TO SERVE Remove the kulfi from the freezer about 5 minutes before serving, just to soften it. Serve in the ceramic bowls (or ramekins). (If using kulfi containers, place each one under warm running water for 30 to 45 seconds, then unscrew the lids and empty the kulfi into individual bowls.)

MEETI ROTI

1 cup all-purpose
flour for rolling

chapatti dough for six
chapattis (page 172), chilled

1 to 3 tsp canola oil
(optional, for rolling)

3 to 4 Tbsp ghee (page 30),
room temperature

8 Tbsp demerara sugar

1¾ oz whole raw,
unsalted cashews, finely
minced but not ground

2 cups kulfi (page 185)

MEETI MEANS "SWEET" and *roti* is the Punjabi word for "chapatti." *Meeti roti* are commonly eaten for brunch or as a breakfast dessert on weekends. The usual version is white sugar stuffed into a chapatti and then cooked with some ghee. It tastes best with raw sugar; however, it is very difficult to cook with raw sugar, as it often comes in solid form and burns very easily. We use demerara sugar instead and add cashews to our meeti roti. You can also use pure maple sugar, although it is very expensive.

Once we roll out the roti and cook it, we pour warm kulfi over it. If you don't have any kulfi, you can also use crème anglaise. Even without kulfi or crème anglaise, meeti roti is great with a cup of coffee or tea. Because you control how much sugar and cashews go into each roti, you can put in however much you choose. Some people, like Vikram, prefer more sugar and cashews, others prefer less. We've given the measurements we use at the restaurant.

Since these roti must be eaten *à la minute*, hot off the grill, you may want to have one person roll out a roti while another person cooks one. If you want to serve each guest a whole roti, be aware that your guests will all be eating at different times. Alternatively, you can cook each roti, cut it in wedges and serve each person a wedge. We serve meeti roti at our Rangoli café and this is, unanimously, the favourite dessert of Vikram and Meeru and our staff.

Serves 6

WHEN YOU ARE ready to start rolling out your roti, heat the *thava* on medium-high heat (if you are using a frying pan, heat it on medium heat) for 5 to 7 minutes.

Spread flour on a flat plate. Divide the chilled dough in six equal portions. Dab one portion in a little flour. Using your hands, roll the dough into a smooth ball. If it is sticky, rub ½ tsp oil on your hands. Once you have a smooth ball, roll it in the flour, covering it completely but lightly. With a rolling pin, roll out the ball until it is 3 to 4 inches in diameter. When the roti starts sticking to your rolling pin, cover both sides of the roti once again in the flour, completely but lightly.

Spread ½ tsp ghee on the rolled-out roti. Spread about 1 Tbsp + 1 tsp sugar over the ghee and about 2 tsp of the minced cashews over the sugar. Rub a little bit of oil on your hands, then gather the edges of the dough and bring them together above the filling. Pat the filled ball to be sure

the filling is tightly enclosed. The shape you end up with doesn't really matter. Some of us make triangles, others make balls. The point is to tightly enclose the filling in the roti.

Carefully roll this shape in the flour, flattening it slightly and covering it completely but lightly. With a rolling pin, roll out until it is 3 to 4 inches in diameter (or the equivalent if you don't have an exact circle), or until it starts to stick to the rolling pin. Dip both sides of the roti in flour again, covering it completely but lightly, and continue rolling until the roti is 8 inches in diameter.

Carefully lift the roti and place it on the hot thava (or frying pan). The roti should be flat, without any folds. Cook roti on one side for about 1 minute, or until little bubbles start to form. You may also hear some sizzling if sugar has leaked from the roti. Using a spatula, turn over the roti. Spread the top with 1 tsp of ghee and cook for another minute. Flip roti over again and spread the top with another 1 tsp of ghee. Continue cooking, 1 minute per side, until roti is golden brown and crispy, with dark patches on both sides. Each roti should take about 4 to 6 minutes to cook completely. (If the sugar begins to burn, then slightly decrease the heat and flip the roti more often. The process is very similar to making a regular chapatti, except that there's no need to fluff the roti since bubbles will appear on their own.) Transfer the cooked roti to a cutting board.

TO SERVE Using a pizza cutter or a large knife, cut each roti in 4 to 6 wedges. Arrange the pieces on a plate and top with ⅓ cup of the kulfi. Repeat this procedure with the remaining 5 portions of dough, until you have cooked all 6 meeti rotis. Use individual plates for each meeti roti with kulfi.

RICE PUDDING

WE GREW UP eating rice pudding, but we started cooking this recipe at the restaurant because it was the simplest dessert to make while we were focussing more on our appetizers and entrées. We believe the main reason it tastes so good is that we use basmati rice. If you don't use basmati rice, your rice pudding will taste nothing like ours. Make sure you buy Indian basmati rice.

The key to good rice pudding is to cook it slowly on low heat and make sure that the milk never sticks to the bottom of the pan. Rice pudding can be eaten as a warm, hot or cold dessert. If you wish to serve it chilled, wait until the pudding is at room temperature before putting it into the refrigerator.

This recipe yields 10 cups of rice pudding. In our household of four, since we eat rice pudding as a breakfast, snack or dessert, this lasts about three days.

Makes 10 cups

10 to 12 green cardamom pods

¾ cup basmati rice

12 cups homogenized milk

1 cup sugar

⅓ cup chopped raw unsalted almonds (peeled or unpeeled)

LIGHTLY POUND green cardamoms and peel off the pods. Empty brownish-black seeds into a medium pot. Discard the pods. Add rice and milk and bring to a gentle boil on medium-low heat. Simmer, stirring gently and regularly, for about 1 hour and 10 minutes. Never scrape the bottom of the pot while stirring, otherwise you may get bits of slightly burned milk in your pudding. As the rice and the milk cook, the consistency will become more and more like pudding. If the rice begins to clump or the milk begins to stick to the bottom of the pan, stir more often or turn down the heat slightly. (The milk burns quickly once it sticks and gives the entire pudding a burnt taste.) Remove the pot from the heat and add sugar. Stir well.

TO SERVE Divide rice pudding among individual bowls. Sprinkle almonds over the pudding just before serving.

FENNEL- AND INDIAN THYME–
CANDIED WALNUTS

½ tsp fennel seeds

½ tsp ajwain seeds

1 tsp salt

¼ tsp ground
cayenne pepper

½ cup ghee (page 30)

1 oz raw sugar

7 oz raw walnut halves
(about 2 cups)

W E USE RAW sugar in this recipe. It usually comes in chunks, so you can't measure it in cups, and can be difficult to crush completely. This recipe is made very quickly, within 10 minutes, but it is crucial that you stir the entire time so the sugar doesn't stick and burn. You must use ghee rather than butter or oil in this recipe.

We serve 4 to 5 candied walnuts on our mildly spiced seafood curries, such as Sturgeon, Mussels and Baby Carrots in Tomato, Light Cream Curry (page 118). These walnuts would clash with some of our more heavily spiced curries like the beef short ribs. They are also delicious and addictive when eaten on their own.

The walnuts will keep in an airtight container in a dark cupboard or drawer for up to 1 month. Make sure you always reseal the container properly after opening, otherwise the walnuts will become stale and the sugar will not remain crispy.

Makes 3 cups

LINE A BAKING tray with either aluminum foil or waxed paper. Combine fennel and ajwain seeds in a small bowl. In another small bowl, combine salt and cayenne.

Melt ghee in a heavy-bottomed frying pan (not nonstick) on medium-high heat. Once ghee has completely melted (about 1 minute), stir in the mixed seeds. Allow them to sizzle for 1½ to 2 minutes, then add the salt and cayenne mixture. Stir well. After 1 minute add sugar, stirring constantly and crushing chunks with a spoon as the sugar melts with the heat. Keep your face away from the pot, in case the sugar splatters a bit. The raw sugar will foam a little and, while it is foaming and cooking, will seem lighter in colour. Once it stops foaming, it will take on a reddish colour. It should take a total of 5 to 8 minutes to melt the sugar entirely.

Once sugar has melted, stir in walnuts. Turn off the heat and immediately pour candied walnuts onto the baking tray, spreading them in a single layer with a spatula, while the sugar is still soft. Allow walnuts to cool and the sugar to harden, then break in 1½-inch pieces with your hands or cut with a thick knife.

MANGO LASSI

LASSI IS A buttermilk or yogurt drink, salty or sweet, that more or less has the consistency of a smoothie. Some people prefer their lassi with more yogurt or buttermilk, others prefer it with more water and/or ice. We make our lassi with yogurt, as some people find cold buttermilk an acquired taste. Although sweet lassis do contain sugar, they are nevertheless a healthy drink and they make a great after-school snack. In India, many people drink salty lassis to cool their body during the summer months.

Since the taste and consistency of a lassi is such a personal preference, it is tempting just to list the ingredients and let you decide for yourself how much of each to add. Instead we are providing two basic recipes that you can then modify as you like. Personally, we like our salty lassis colder, so we have added more ice cubes to that recipe. Depending on the quality of your blender, you may not be able to completely crush all of the ice cubes. Don't mix the lassi in the blender for more than two minutes, as it becomes too frothy.

You can buy Alphonse mango pulp (page 159) with no preservatives or artificial flavours. Although we add a touch of pineapple to complement and balance the sweetness of the pulp, it is optional. If you do decide to add the pineapple, buy freshly cut fruit, as the unsweetened canned variety can be tart and sweetened canned pineapple is too sweet. You will need a blender to mix all the ingredients.

We normally drink lassi on its own and not with a meal, as it is quite filling.

Makes 4 servings (12 ounces each)

SWEET LASSI Combine yogurt, mango pulp, sugar, pineapple (if desired), water and ice cubes in a blender. Cover and mix (or crush) for about 45 seconds, or until you no longer hear the ice cubes crushing. Pour immediately into glasses and serve.

SALTY LASSI Combine yogurt, salt, black pepper, water and ice cubes in a blender. Cover and mix (or crush) for about 1 minute, or until you no longer hear the ice cubes crushing. Pour immediately into glasses and serve.

SWEET LASSI

2 cups yogurt

1½ cups Alphonse mango pulp

4 Tbsp sugar

3 oz fresh pineapple (optional)

2 cups water

5 or 6 ice cubes

SALTY LASSI

2 cups yogurt

1 tsp salt

½ tsp ground black pepper

2 cups water

7 or 8 ice cubes

VIJ'S CHAI

N DECEMBER 1994, when we had our very first lineup in our then fourteen-seat restaurant, Vikram hurried to the kitchen and made cups of chai (which means simply a cup of tea with milk) for the four or five customers who were waiting. It struck him as rude that they would wait without being offered anything as a welcome or a thank you. In India, it is unheard of for anyone to come to your home without being offered a cup of tea or (relatively recently) coffee. Chai also goes very well with Indian desserts or as an after-dinner drink in place of dessert.

After that evening, Meeru determined to figure out how to make chai that would always be fresh and piping hot for customers waiting for tables. If it is too milky, chai gets a coating of milk if it stays on the heat for long. Likewise, if we use spices like cinnamon or cloves, they become too strong and bitter if the tea stays on the burner for any length of time. In North America, there are also many requests that are unheard of in India—most notably, "no milk, please" or "no sugar, please." If someone asks for chai with no milk (which often happens at Vij's), then they're not drinking what Indians refer to as chai.

There are so many variations that an entire book could be written on ways to make chai. We once witnessed a passionate discussion between Vikram's father and Meeru's mother on which brand of teabag was the best replacement for the loose tea they used in India. In India the most notable difference is between the chai people from villages drink and the type those from the cities drink. Our kitchen staff drinks what we call "Punjabi chai," which is like a latte with mostly milk and sugar and relatively little tea. They make it in one big pot and serve it once the milk is almost boiling. In the winter, they add ajwain, ginger or black cardamom to their chai to prevent colds. You can't keep a batch of Punjabi chai going: you must make it and drink it right away. Meeru and Vikram grew up with "city chai," which has mostly water and tea, with less milk and sugar. We also add mild spices such as green cardamom and fennel seeds. We can keep a pot of it going, with the spices and teabags taken out once the chai is made, and then add the milk to each cup.

Makes 6 cups

12 to 15 green cardamom pods

5½ cups water

1½ tsp fennel seeds

6 tsp sugar

5 orange pekoe teabags

¾ cup milk

PLACE A SMALL bowl and tea strainer beside the stove. With a knife or your hands, peel the green cardamom skins halfway so you can see the seeds inside. In a kettle or a large pot, combine water, cardamom pods, fennel and sugar, stir once, then bring to a boil on medium-high heat. As soon as water starts to boil vigorously, add teabags. Stir once and boil for 1 minute, or 1½ minutes for slightly stronger tea. Using a spoon, remove teabags and place them in the bowl. Discard these later.

If everyone is having chai with milk, reduce the heat to medium and add milk. Heat for 30 to 45 seconds, then turn off heat. Place the tea strainer over each cup individually and fill. You should have enough to fill six cups. Be careful, as this is very hot chai.

If someone in your group doesn't want milk in their tea, you can warm the milk separately and add it to each cup accordingly. Remember that you will then need to use extra water and less milk than is listed in the ingredients.

GINGER-LEMON DRINK

½ cup fresh lemon or
lime juice (about 3 juicy
lemons or limes)

4 oz ginger, unpeeled, or
¼ cup fresh ginger juice

5 Tbsp sugar or to taste

6 bottles (each 250 mL) still
or sparkling water, chilled

6 sprigs of mint (optional)

W E CAME UP with this recipe ten years ago, when we didn't have a liquor licence at our original location and wanted a special drink that went particularly well with Indian food. Indians tend to choose a still-water drink with their food, whereas we find that North Americans tend to enjoy a carbonated drink, even if it is water. For this drink, we leave the choice of still or sparkling water up to you.

Although we call this drink Ginger-Lemon, we also use limes if the lemons are not juicy enough. It is important to have juicy lemons or limes and young, fat ginger—make sure the ginger isn't skinny, with wrinkled skin. If you can't find thin-skinned, juicy lemons or limes, buy the regular, thick-skinned lemons, poke them with a knife and place them in the microwave for 3 minutes on high. Allow them to cool for a minute, then squeeze out the lemon juice. The amount of juice you extract from the lemons and ginger will depend on their quality. You will need a grater or a juicer to extract the juice from the ginger. The sweet/tart flavours of your lemon or lime, as well as the amount of bitterness in your ginger (some fresh ginger will be sweeter and more "gingery," whereas other fresh ginger will have a more bitter aftertaste) will determine exactly how much you need. The quantities we use always vary slightly, depending on the qualities of the produce.

Create this drink the way you like it. Some people prefer a sweeter drink and others prefer a slightly less sweet drink, so adjust the amount of sugar to your preference. In India, many people prefer a saltier ginger-lemon drink. A sprig of mint tastes great during the afternoon, especially if the sun is out. It's fine in the evenings as well, but here in Vancouver, many evenings are wet and dark and fresh mint doesn't reflect the required coziness.

The concentrate will keep in an airtight container for 3 to 4 days in the refrigerator or for 1 month in the freezer.

Makes 6 cups

STRAIN LEMON (or lime) juice through a large fine-mesh sieve into a measuring cup. Using a large ladle or a cooking spoon, lightly press lemon (or lime) pulp through the sieve to extract as much juice as possible. Discard solids but reserve the juice. You should have about ½ cup.

The easiest way to get ginger juice is to peel the ginger, discard the skin and put the root through a juicer. If you do not have a juicer, thoroughly wash the unpeeled ginger. Using a hand grater, grate ginger into

a bowl. Scoop ginger into one hand, make a tight fist and squeeze, allowing juice to run into the bowl. (You can also place grated ginger on a
square of cheesecloth, twist it closed and squeeze the ginger juice out of
it.) Strain ginger juice through the sieve and into the measuring cup with
the lemon juice.

Add sugar to the ginger-lemon juice and stir with a spoon until sugar
dissolves completely, about 3 minutes.

TO SERVE Divide the ginger-lemon concentrate among six glasses.
Top up with sparkling or still water. Garnish with a sprig of mint. (At Vij's,
we serve the concentrate in small individual glass containers. Customers
pour the concentrate into individual glasses and add 1 cup or more
water to taste.)

METRIC CONVERSION CHART
(rounded off to the nearest even whole number)

WEIGHT

IMPERIAL OR U.S.	METRIC
1 oz	30 g
2 oz	60 g
3 oz	85 g
4 oz	115 g
5 oz	140 g
6 oz	170 g
7 oz	200 g
8 oz (½ lb)	225 g
9 oz	255 g
10 oz	285 g
11 oz	310 g
12 oz	340 g
13 oz	370 g
14 oz	400 g
15 oz	425 g
16 oz (1 lb)	455 g
2 lbs	910 g

VOLUME

IMPERIAL OR U.S.	METRIC
⅛ tsp	0.5 mL
¼ tsp	1 mL
½ tsp	2.5 mL
¾ tsp	4 mL
1 tsp	5 mL
1 Tbsp	15 mL
1½ Tbsp	23 mL
⅛ cup	30 mL
¼ cup	60 mL
⅓ cup	80 mL
½ cup	120 mL
⅔ cup	160 mL
¾ cup	180 mL
1 cup	240 mL

ACKNOWLEDGEMENTS

THE SEED FOR VIJ'S was planted in Amritsar in the 1970s by Roshan Lal Vij, my *Daddy ji* and paternal grandfather. Daddy ji loved to sit on his veranda in the evenings, with me at his side, drink his Scotch and water, smoke his cigarettes and eat dinner from his pure silver bowls and plates. His dinner had to be presented beautifully. With the gentle, yet constant complaints of my grandmother in the background, Daddy ji would always say to me, "One day, you and I will open up a five-star restaurant with a bar. I will be your main customer and we won't let your grandmother enter."

Vij's Restaurant is named after Roshan Lal, who died many years before Vij's opened. My fondest childhood memories are of my summers in Amritsar. I spent every day sneaking to the candy stores and food vendors down the street, and walking through all the alleyways with my grandmother on our daily trip to the temple and the shops. My evenings were spent with my grandfather, patiently waiting for the whisky to take effect so that I could ask for more money for the next day's secret sweets and snacks.

My grandmother, Sarla Vij, who died of cancer in August 1994, knew that my parents were coming to Canada for three months to help me open a new restaurant. She told my father not to spend any more time with her, to say his final goodbyes and to get to Vancouver as soon as possible. She didn't want to delay my future. My parents, Manmohan and Kusum Vij, took heed of her request and arrived here as planned, with an energy that only parental love can fuel. And for this they will always have my gratitude and love.

I also want to thank my extended family—the entire staff at Vij's—and in particular Amarjeet Gill, our kitchen manager, and Mike Bernardo, our general manager and wine director. They keep things going with enthusiasm and commitment, as if Vij's was their very own restaurant.

Vikram Vij

MY FATHER'S FAVOURITE joke is that he paid thousands of dollars for my university education, just so that I could get married and become a glorified cook. He starts chuckling even before he finishes the joke, while my sister and mother chime right in with their laughter. My sister will then carry on with her favourite joke, which is that I am making money by copying Mom's recipes, and that Vikram and I owe Mom royalties. They repeat these jokes during every trip to Vancouver and to Vij's. Best of all, after all these years, these quips can still make the four of us laugh like crazy. Behind our laughter is great pride and camaraderie, and I thank them for it.

In particular I would also like to thank Amarjeet Gill, who is the backbone in our kitchen. I fell for her big smile the first time I met her at Vij's, and it was with her support that I began experimenting with the food. Early on, we also hired another Amarjeet Gill, only this one was older and we called her *Aunty*. Aunty had just moved to Canada from her village in the Punjab. She and I could have come from two different planets, but she turned out to be my cooking kindred spirit and we are now like mother and daughter.

As for my own mother, Omi, who lives in Virginia, she is my good-luck charm in life. She is also my cooking encyclopedia and a constant source of new ideas. More than half of the recipes in this book have benefitted from Omi's input.

I want to thank Sital Dale, who worked tirelessly with me to cook every single recipe in this book. Whereas you have the English version of our recipes, Sital has meticulously written the Punjabi version in her notebook. And, of course, Sital would not have been able to work with me if Paramjeet (Jaya) Sandhu had not done such a fine job of taking over the cooking with Amarjeet.

Meeru Dhalwala

INDEX